Luxembourg: The Clog-Shaped Duchy

A Chronological History of Luxembourg from the Celts to the Present Day

authorHOUSE

1663 LIBERTY DRIVE, SUITE 200
BLOOMINGTON, INDIANA 47403
(800) 839-8640
WWW.AUTHORHOUSE.COM

© 2005 Andrew Reid. All Rights Reserved.

No part of this book may be reproduced, stored in a retrieval system, or transmitted by any means without the written permission of the author.

First published by AuthorHouse 11/28/05

ISBN: 1-4259-0189-1 (sc)

Printed in the United States of America
Bloomington, Indiana

This book is printed on acid-free paper.

Introduction

Luxembourg is one of the world's smallest states. Yet despite its size it was one of the great powers of the Western world, its influence reaching as far as Lithuania and the Czech Republic of today. Its heyday was from the twelfth to the fifteenth century but even beyond its apex it remains a fascinating study for the historian. Its history is a microcosm of Europe, every ripple and current impacting on this tiny nation. The architecture of the country shows evidence of layer upon layer of invader and conqueror; from Roman and Celtic relics, to Frankish and medieval forts and castles and later, grander fortifications from the French and Spanish. From Luxembourg arose crusaders and brutal princes as well enlightened reformers, such as the Empress Ermesinde. It was on Luxembourg's soil that great religious currents took root. In later centuries, its own rulers long gone, Luxembourg became a pawn in the great game of European history, passed from dynasty to dynasty. And for most of this time the people of Luxembourg watched from the sidelines, preserving their own culture, way of life and folklore. In the nineteenth century Luxembourg began to emerge as a small economic power in its own right, giving rise to artists, industrial magnates and writers. Having come through the crucible of two world wars and two invasions, Luxembourg found its role as a founding member of the new Europe, with influence and international prestige way beyond its size. What follows is the story of Luxembourg.

Chapter One: Ancient tribes, Romans, rocky castles and saints: The Beginnings of Lucilinburhuc

Human settlement has been present in Luxembourg from the very dawn of humanity. One of the very earliest traces of human settlement in Luxembourg is Magdalenian Man who was discovered near the town of Oetrange. Mesolithic and megalithic remains have also been unearthed by archaeologists in the Grand Duchy. However, our narrative of the history of Luxembourg really begins much later. Like much of northern Europe, Luxembourg in the time before Rome was settled by tribes of Celts, a race of people with origins in the Iberian peninsular. Their religion evolved into what is now known as Druidism. Wild Druid priests lurked in the thick forests of pine that covered the land. Strange rituals and sacrifices coexisted with a vibrant and rich culture, advanced in the skills of jewellery making and creative arts. There were refuges for Druid priests in the Mullerthal valley and on the Titelberg, and Widenberg hills, where sacrifices were performed. To this day a Celtic monument survives near the village of Altlinster, which consists of a mutilated figure cut into rock. Sometimes known as the Rock of Hertha, or as *De Man an de Frau op der Lei* in Luxemburgish, the monument is a lewd fertility symbol.

However, the Celts were not alone. Also in the area were two Belgian tribes, the Treveri, who lived near the present German city of Trier, just across the river Moselle, and the Mediomatrici tribe, who lived near the present day French city of Metz. The tribes were fiercely loyal to their own, and brutal and tenacious in the face of invasion. Such loyalty and grit were vital for survival in that brutal world where exclusion from the group meant certain death, either from hunger or from the packs of wolves who shared the land with its human inhabitants.

However to the south of Luxembourg a new and powerful force was massing, and in 53 BCE the Roman legions of Julius Caesar conquered Gaul and the territory which is now Luxembourg. The Treveri fought bravely and their leader, Indutiomar, died in battle, probably on the banks of the Alzette river. What happened to the survivors is unclear but for many their fate was slavery at the hands of the Romans.

Following their victory the Romans settled on the highly strategic position in what is now the Grand Duchy, attracted by fertile valleys and timber rich hills. They also added their own fortress to the Celtic ruins. The rocky gorges made ideal forts and the location secured the routes from the Roman settlement of Trier into France. The Romans built four principal forts in Luxembourg. One excavated fort was that of Dalheim in the south of the country, the others were at Helperknap, Alttrier and the old Celtic Titelberg site.

The Romans carved straight and efficient roads across the land, one of them being under the present-day Grand rue, the fashionable thoroughfare at the heart of Luxembourg City. In the *Antonine Itinerary* there is record of a rest stop on one such road referred to as Andethana, which corresponds to the present-day town of Niederanven. This marked the half-way point of the Arlon-Trier route, the former town being known as Oralaunum.

To this day Roman remains are to be found all over

the Grand Duchy, notably in Diekirsch and Echternach. There are remains of a Roman bridge at Stadtbredimus and of Roman river works on the Moselle river. There is also recorded Roman settlement in Mondorf, the town sitting strategically on the Trier-Metz (Divodurum) road, as well of traces of a Roman town at Remich which was called Remacum by the Romans. The village of Christnach, near Larochette was known to the Romans as Crucenacum and significant Roman remains were found there. Another famous Luxembourgish town, Wasserbillig, was in fact the Roman Bilacus and it was here that the famous Column of Igel was built, reaching 75 meters, and proclaiming Roman imperial might to all who passed by. The town of Dalheim was known as Ricciacum. A Roman altar was unearthed at the Niederburg forest not far from Echternach, possibly dedicated to the goddess Diana, and near Bollendorf a stone in honour of Mercury was excavated. The church in the village of Berdorf has an altar upon which are reliefs of Hercules, Apollo, Juno and Minerva illustrating how Roman religion was incorporated quite readily into early Christianity.

Roman influence increased substantially as Trier grew into one of the most important towns in the Roman Empire, crowned with its still surviving Porta Negra arch. There is even evidence of early Roman commuters in the town of Echternach, who built villas in the hills around the town. One of the Roman forts was built near the present day *Bock* in Luxembourg City during the reign of Gallienus, and became known as Lucilinburhuc, meaning 'small castle.'

There is evidence of substantial Roman settlement and civilisation in Luxembourg, illustrating that there was a comfortable and settled way of life in the land and not just a military presence. An example of this is the remains of well-preserved Roman mosaics near Diekirch and at Medernach. The mosaics depict, in frightening detail, the two-faced mythological figure Medusa.

Luxembourg provided Rome with plentiful supplies of timber, and there is evidence that the Romans exploited iron ore. It is also believed that Luxembourgish hams and wines were delicacies much in demand in Rome and were praised by the poet Ausonius. Ausonius was a teacher to the son of Emperor Valentinien and he wrote a long epic poem known as *Mosella* in which he lauds the wine of the area.

By the 4th century however, the Roman Empire was falling apart, being over stretched and decadent. The Romans had never quite managed to stamp out the Celtic and Treveri spirit of independence in the conquered land, despite officially banning the Druid religion. During this time there were some recorded attempts at making converts by early Christians and an ancient shrine to St Quirinus in the Pétrusse valley dates from this era. Facing pressures from inside and out the Roman occupation of Luxembourg was drawing to a close. Eventually the Romans needed to pull out their troops in order to defend Rome itself, leaving the area vulnerable.

This represented rich pickings for the marauding Huns who were sweeping west, culminating in raids by Attila the Hun around 450 CE. To this day Attila is remembered in the town name Ettelbruck, a derivation meaning Attila's bridge. Various tribes swept the land including the Alans, the Vandals, the Visigoths and Suevi.

The area eventually fell under the control of the

Rheinland Franks, as part of the kingdom of Austrasia. Many small towns and rural settlements sprang up during this period and it was the Franks who gave some Luxembourgish places their present names, for example Muomendorph, which later became Mondorf. It was during this period that the Luxembourgish language, Letzebuergesch, began to evolve as a fusion of French and Moselle-German. During the fifth century a castle was built at Vianden in an effort to consolidate Frankish rule, a place which was to take on great significance in later centuries. Frankish tombs were later unearthed at Emmeringen and Waldwies.

By the beginning of the 6th century the Frankish settlement was complete and a powerful leader, Clovis, had consolidated himself as the established ruler. It was Clovis who was largely responsible for the partial introduction of Christianity, becoming one of the earliest converts to the new faith in 496. Nevertheless it would take a few more centuries before the land became fully Christianised. During this time a certain fusion of pagan and Druid culture took place with basic Christian tenets acquiring pagan trappings. Indeed to this day the forests and hills of Luxembourg have a faintly dark feel illustrated for example by the sale of little witch and troll souvenirs and the survival of ancient superstitions. Restaurants and bars are often decorated with broomsticks and every year, in the depths of winter, Carnival is celebrated, hinting back to a pagan past.

From the late 5th century began the so-called Merovingian period under the descendants of Clovis. During this period, law was the product of custom rather than royal decree, and the main powerbrokers were the *graf* or counts. The next layer up from the counts were the *duces,* who commanded larger districts, and at the head of this power structure was the king of the Franks.

It is at this point in our narrative that we come across an enigmatic Anglo-Saxon saint, an English-born Christian missionary, who founded one of Western Europe's greatest abbeys in the Luxembourgish town of Echternach. His name was Willibrord. Willibrord was originally from the Yorkshire town of Ripon but he was taken into exile in Ireland by his father. It was in Ireland that Willibrord became a priest and towards the end of the seventh century he and twelve companions set off to the land of Frisia, now part of the Netherlands, to convert the pagans living there to Christianity. The land was under the control of Pepin II and was constantly being fought over. However, Willibrod's Benedictine mission prospered and his work was given a boost when he received the backing of Pope Sergius. This followed Willibrord's pilgrimage to Rome, an enormous feat of courage and determination in the seventh century. After a second pilgrimage to Rome in 695 he was made a bishop. Willibrord returned to Frisia and to his base in Utrecht. From here Willibrord set about ordaining priests and bishops to cater to the newly Christianised peoples of the area. It is in 698 that Willibrord founded the abbey at Echternach, which was his largest and most important.

At the turn of the seventh century another figure emerged, Hubert of Maastricht. He too spread the gospel in the Ardennes region and built a cathedral at the city of Liege, now in Belgium. A rocky pulpit in the park at Clervaux is also attributed to him.

Hubert is said to have been hunting when a stag appeared with a cross between its antlers. This caused

Hubert to desist from his hunt, and he henceforth took upon himself a life of piety, giving up his earthly honours.

Meanwhile, Willibrord's work suffered a set back when Utrecht was taken over by a hostile pagan king, Radbod, who destroyed the newly built churches Willibrord had built. On Radbod's death in 719 Willibrord returned not only to Utrecht but also to other non-Christianised areas of the Netherlands where he converted large numbers of pagans to the new faith. Willibrord even penetrated Norse Denmark where he killed holy cows and destroyed idols, putting his own life at risk. However this act, which was almost certainly inspired by the actions of the biblical Elija, served its purpose and shocked the pagans into conversion.

Willibrord was joined in his work by another Anglo-Saxon priest, Winfrith Boniface. Like Willibrord, Boniface chose to work spreading Christianity in Frisia and the Netherlands. Boniface arrived in the Netherlands in 716 but he returned to England due to the unstable political climate. Like Willibrord he made the arduous and perilous journey to Rome where he received the support of Pope Gregory II in 718. Boniface then began work in Germany, although he also supported Willibrord in the Netherlands. Like Willibrord he too destroyed pagan idols. Boniface then moved on to the area of Metz to the south of the present-day Grand Duchy. Boniface eventually returned to Frisia where he met a violent death and was subsequently canonised.

Back in the Netherlands and Luxembourg Willibrord became famous for his purported powers for curing epilepsy and became something of a cult figure. He was known as a gracious and joyful man, who devoted himself to study, reflection and prayer. He was a great evangelist and Echternach was not the only abbey to flourish. Many monasteries sprang up all over newly Christianised Luxembourg, for example the monasteries of Prum and St Hubert, providing people with basic education and sometimes with primitive cures.

It was in the monasteries that ancient Roman culture, language and texts were preserved. Remains of the ancient church at Diekirch date back to this era. In 727 Hubert died and was subsequently canonised. Willibrord died around 740 at the age of 81 and was buried at his abbey in Echternach. This became and has remained to this day an important place of pilgrimage, especially when Willibrord became the patron saint of the Netherlands in later years. Gradually, over the centuries, a ritual evolved focusing on the shrine of Willibrord in Echternach. This became known as the *Springprozession* and to this day it takes place annually on Whit Tuesday. Upwards of 15,000 pilgrims gather in the town from all over the Low Countries. It is accompanied by dancing and music, which soon becomes a feast and a street party.

In 752 the last of the Merovingians kings was deposed, the line gradually becoming weak in the face of the ascending Carolingian dynasty. Pepin the Short was elected as king of the Franks and as such became the first of the Carolingians to rule the land. In 768 Pepin's son Charlemagne became king and he made the German town of Aachen, not far from the present Grand Duchy, his capital. The proximity of Aachen to Luxembourg put the area well and truly onto the map. This had ramifications for centuries to come and was both a blessing and a curse. In addition to being King of the Franks, Charlemagne became the Holy Roman Emperor a few years later in 800. Charlemagne married Hildegarde from the Thionville, now in northern France, and the territory of present day Luxembourg lay half way between Charlemagne's capital Aachen and the new Empress's hometown. Consequently a number of new settlements sprang up, and Charlemagne built himself a palace near the present day town of Mondorf where he could break his journey.

In 843 the Treaty of Verdun partitioned Charlemagne's empire between his three grandsons. Under the treaty Luxembourg was given to Lothair as part of the so-called Middle Kingdom. In 855 Lothair died and was succeeded by Lothair II and at this point the Middle Kingdom became known as Lotharingia, another name for Lorraine. The Kingdom of Lotharingia remained under the protection of the Holy Roman Empire, such as it was. A further carving up of the empire took place at the Treaty of Mersen, in 870 and then again in 925, when the territory of Luxembourg came under German control and into the clutches of Henry the Fowler.

Chapter Two: Siegfried and the Luxembourg Dynasty

Most nations have myths about their origins and Luxembourg is no exception, with a host of romantic legends surrounding a certain count named Siegfried. Siegfried of Lorraine or Sigefroi as he is often called, was the youngest of the Counts of the Ardennes and is regarded as Luxembourg's founder. In one myth Siegfried sold his soul to the Devil, and it was Satan himself who built Luxembourg's castle in a single night. A more romantic and flattering account describes Siegfried coming across a young maiden on the banks of the Alzette river combing her hair. Siegfried married her and in return the maiden built her husband the castle, similarly in one night. The maiden's name was Melusine and she had only one condition attached to her gift of the castle. She asked that Saturday be her own private day. For years Siegfried respected her wish and let her be but eventually he gave in to his burning curiosity. He followed her to the Alzette valley and watched her bathe. Melusine was in fact a mermaid, a punishment she incurred for having enclosed her father in a mountain. When she turned to see Siegfried standing behind her, Melusine vanished into the rock where she remains to this day. Indeed, the French still use the expression *un cri de Mélusine* to describe a shout of shock and anguish. According to the legend Melusine knits a stitch a year, awaiting a brave man to release her by taking the key from a snake. The myth states that such a man will secure the entire wealth of Luxembourg. Should he fail however, or should Melusine finish her knitting then all of Luxembourg will vanish into the rocks.

A more likely account is that in 963 Count Siegfried, husband of Hedwig Modgau, exchanged some of his land for an old Roman fortress, guarding the Alzette valley. This fortress had been built on the site of a bridge on the old Roman road that ran from Paris to Trier. Siegfried then built fortifications around it, creating the core of the future Luxembourg City and carving himself a semi-independent land within the Holy Roman Empire. His fortifications were concentrated on the *Rocher du Bock*, which he bought from the Abbey of St Maximin of Trier on April 12th 963. The castle, standing at 1065 feet above sea level, became the basis of the present-day *Casemates*, a warren of cave-like defences. At their strongest, the fortifications boasted twenty four forts, a network of tunnels that totalled nearly fifteen miles, and three ring walls. The fortifications were tested in 984 when the castle was besieged.

In 987 the church of St Michel was built as the castle chapel and a church has remained on this site ever since.

On 28th October 998 Siegried died and was replaced by Henry I who ruled until 1026. Siegfried and his descendants gave rise to many of the royal families of Europe.

Sirgfried also had a daughter, Kunigunde. Kunigunde married Heinrich IV of Bavaria and was crowned queen of Paderborn in 1002. On St Valentine's day 1014 Kunigunde was proclaimed Empress along with her husband, the new Emperor. However in 1017 Heinrich died and a childless and distraught Kunigunde withdrew herself into a convent, where she died in 1039. During her stay at the convent Kunigunde reputedly walked unscathed over red-hot ploughshares, a feat for she was canonised in 1200.

In 1000 Boursheid Castle was built on hills, surrounded by thick forest. The craggy remains of Boursheid castle remain to this day one of the enduring images of the Grand Duchy. This was to be followed soon after by other castles which came to dominate the landscape and the people who lived in their shadows.

In 1016 the abbey at Echtenach, which had been built by St Willibrord, burned down and a new imposing church was built in its place. This new Romanesque abbey was begun in 1017 but was not completed until 1037. The abbey soon became one of the most important centres of learning in Christendom with much of the work being carried out by English monks. It was here that the monks carefully copied manuscripts by hand in beautiful lettering, taking years to complete their labours of love. One of the most important manuscripts to emerge from Echternach was the *Codex Aureus Epternacenis,* an incredibly ornate book of gospel.

In October of the year 1019 Frederic I count of Luxembourg and son of Siegfried died. Meanwhile, Henry I remained in charge of Luxembourg.

In 1026 Henry II became king and ruled until 1047. He was replaced by Giselbert who ruled until his death on 14th August 1059. It was under Giselbert's rule that the original Three Towers in the Pfaffenthal were built in 1050 to mark the outer limits of the city walls. It is also during Giselbert's reign that the famous monastery of Orval was established, now in Belgian Luxembourg.

By 1083, under the reign of Conrad I, local warlords were using the title of *Graf von Lutzelburg* or the Counts of Luxembourg. This was a step towards a sense of Luxembourgish identity.

Conrad was replaced in 1086 by Henry III. Then, and until 1126, the land was ruled by Conrad II. Conrad II is known to have made visits to the great Abbey at Echternach to secure religious approval.

During this period Luxembourg developed into a feudal state. The castle at Clervaux dates from this time, when a certain Gerard of Clervaux bought himself a small parcel of highly strategic land and built a little fortress. Also dating from this time is the town of Esch-sur-Alzette, which was first recorded in a Papal Bull of 1128.

Other castles followed during the twelfth century including Esch-sur-Sure, Hollenfels and Bouillon, which was lost to Luxembourg when the country was partitioned hundreds of years later. The castles were an integral part of the feudal system with a lord or count ruling over serfs and peasants who lived in the small villages under the shadow of the castles. It was the lords who dispensed their own, and often very rough, justice.

The castle of Esch-sur-Sure in particular has a grizzly legend, which dates back to the 12th century. A knight from Esch is said to have returned to the town from a crusade bearing a macabre souvenir. In his hand was the severed head of a Turk. Feeling frightfully pleased with himself the knight hung his trophy from the gate of the castle. The next day the head had vanished. However, it is believed to return to warn residents of impending disaster ever since. The last time it returned, according to locals, was prior to the German invasion in 1940. Luxembourg is said to have over a hundred such castles and each one is of course haunted.

The imposing fortress at Vianden was completed in the 12th century and became the home of the Counts of Vianden who ruled until loosing sway to the Counts of Luxembourg in 1264. The castles at Beaufort, Roth and Wiltz also date from this era. The Counts of Wiltz in particular were a renowned and powerful dynasty and their tombs exist to this day in the small church at Wiltz. The counts who inhabited Beaufort were also feared, and a torture chamber from their heyday survives in the ruin of their castle.

It was from these castles that Luxembourgish knights sallied forth on the first crusades, foremost amongst them Godfrey of Bouillon, who founded the Kingdom of Jerusalem, in Palestine. These knights included Henri d'Eich who had his own castle on the Sure. Heringerburg Castle, known in English as the Templars Castle, is another relic of the crusaders. Crusading knights often became crippled with debts which they incurred in the Holy Land and on their return they attempted to squeeze every last penny from their serfs. This resulted in great hardships and even famine.

In 1136 Siegfried's line came to an end and the Count of Namur, Heinrich IV, became the Count of Luxembourg. He became known as Henry the Blind of Namur. His territory included not only Luxembourg but also the lands of Namur.

In turn Henry the Blind was replaced in 1196 by the Countess Ermesinde of Arlon, who was based at Poilvache. However Ermesinde was a minor on her accession. Her father dead, the lands she had inherited were in danger of being swallowed up by powerful neighbours. Ermesinde therefore made the wise move of getting married to a powerful protector, Theobold of Bar. Theobold was in fact a descendant of Siegfried and it is he who gave his name to the present-day Belgian town of Bar-le-Duc.

Not only was Ermesinde's inheritance now secured, Theobold added some lands of his own, notably Durbuy and Laroche. Theobold then died and the still young widow Ermesinde married again, this time to Waleran of Limburg. Waleran added the lands of Arlon to those already in the couple's hands. Then, for the second time, Ermesinde lost a husband when Waleran died in 1225.

Upon Waleran's death Ermesinde became the effective leader of Luxembourg, and made her mark by careful government and reform. She was able to centralise power away from the feudal lords by forming a Council of State, based on officers of the court. Until then there had been a kind of rule by 'alpha male' with powerful knights vying for power, often by ruthless means. Using the Council of State she was able to carry out reforms, to a certain degree over the heads of the powerful feudal lords.

Her reforms were wide ranging. She removed the hereditary nature of functional officers, making the position more competitive. She created a court of feudal justice. She also brought towns and villages under her own authority further removing power from the feudal lords in their castles, which must have been a blessed relief indeed for their inhabitants. Moreover it began a process of urbanisation and allowed for the creation of an artisan class, removed from the virtual slave state of feudalism. Under her rule the towns of Thionville, Luxembourg, and Echternach were given charters and thus a degree of independence from the counts. Ermesinde went far in bringing an element of rudimentary justice to the people. For the first time the common people were allowed to access courts in civil matters, although criminal justice remained the privilege of the lords. Peasants became free to move and to own some property. The notorious *droit du seigneur* was limited. Until then a lord had been allowed to deflower any bride before her husband could marry her. Ermesinde also set about creating a range of charitable institutions, schools and monasteries for the benefit of her people, for example the nunnery of Marienthal in 1237. Ermesinde ruled until 1247. By the time of her death Ermesinde had gone a long way in creating a functioning state.

From 1247 until 1281 the land was ruled by Henry V of Limburg, Ermesinde's son and it was he who founded the dynasty of Luxembourg-Limburg.

Henry V was followed by Henry VI who ruled until 1288. It was during Henry VI's reign that the Luxembourgish coat of arms was adopted. It was also under his reign that the first Jews settled in Luxembourg. Henry VI was married to Beatrice who bore him two sons. One of them, Baldwin, was destined to become Archbishop of Trier. The other, Henry, was to rule in his father's footsteps.

In 1288 Henry VI was involved in the battle of Worringen, which was to decide the succession to the Duchy of Limburg. Henry was killed and Limburg was taken by John I, Duke of Brabant.

Following his father's death Henry VII became ruler of Luxembourg. Henry VII was a widely regarded prince. He was wise, forward thinking and above all a good leader. In 1308 Henry VII, with the help of his brother Baldwin, the Archbishop of Trier, was crowned Holy Roman Emperor at the Lateran Palace in Rome. This election was assisted by another powerful Luxembourger, the Archbishop-Prince-Elector of Mainz, Pierre d'Aspelt.

For the two years that he ruled as Emperor, Henry VII did not disappoint his subjects. However in an attempt to unite the Empire he made an ill-fated expedition to Italy where he caught malaria and died in 1310. He was buried in the Cathedral of Pisa in Italy. A more sinister explanation for his death however, is that he was poisoned when taking the sacraments by a treacherous Florentine Guelph.

    Henry's son Jan, aged 14, became the count of Luxembourg in 1310 and then married Elizabeth of Bohemia. As a result of this marriage Jan was crowned king of Bohemia in 1312, there being no male heir to the Bohemian throne, and he became the first of four Luxembourgish kings to rule that land. This connection between Luxembourg and Bohemia can be witnessed at the castle of Karlstejn in the present day Czech Republic where a Luxembourgish coat of arms adorns the wall. As Jan was just 17, the title of Emperor could only be granted to him upon the death of his father, Henry the VI. During his reign Jan went on to fight numerous battles and wars, being a pugnacious man. Indeed he spent nearly every season on the warpath, reputedly only spending four springs at home out of the thirty years of his reign. He fought campaigns in Belgium, Italy and the Baltic, achieving victory after victory. However his luck ran out and he was blinded in one eye during a battle in Lithuania.

    The reason for him being in Lithuania at all were complex. Jan wanted to secure the Hungarian crown for himself. To this end he needed to obtain the support of the Great Teutonic Order, a fanatical group of Germanic knights who were intent on subduing the still semi-pagan Kingdom of Lithuania. To curry their favour he then launched a series of so-called crusades against the Baltic nation. It is on the third such expedition that he lost his eye. Henceforth he would be known as Jan or John the Blind.

Like Ermesinde before him, Jan improved his kingdom, building numerous churches, for example the Church of St Michael in 1320, and by granting municipal charters, accelerating and consolidating the creation of an artisan class. It is during this period that Thomas of Septfontaines founded an important gothic church in his hometown in 1317. In 1328 Jan gave Esch-sur-Alzette the status of free town. He also commissioned a third ring of walls around the capital. He established the Schueberfouer, a fair which was to be held every St Bartholomew's Day and attracted merchants from all over the region. Thus we can see the development of an urban trade-based economy. Jan was a keen traveller and lavish spender, and during his reign he began to accumulate many debts. He was also an arch-schemer, his tactics having been compared to those of the Italian master of ruse, Machiavelli.

However, despite his cunning, many of Jan's projects did not materialise, for instance his planned crusade to the Middle East, his goal of securing Carinthia and Tyrol for Luxembourg or his aim of becoming king of Poland and Hungary. He also began to neglect his Bohemian provinces, which were far from the cultural centres of Europe. By 1340 Jan had become totally blind. This did not however deter him from fighting on behalf of the French king Philip VI against the English. In 1346 Jan was killed at the battle of Crécy. His foe, Edward III, was said to have been distraught at his adversary's death. According to legend Edward picked three ostrich feathers from Jan's helmet and adopted the motto *Ich dien* meaning 'I serve.' The motto and the feathers are still used in the coat of arms the Prince of Wales in the United Kingdom. Jan the Blind is today buried in the Cathedral in Luxembourg City.

It is around this time that the Count of Clervaux built a small chapel dedicated to the three virgins, a small local shrine in the north of the country. This soon developed into a Franciscan church and is the origin of the present day town of Troisvierges.

Following Jan's death at Crécy, his son Charles was crowned Emperor of the Holy Roman Empire. Jan's third son Wenceslas had been in line to inherit Luxembourg, however this was usurped by Charles IV, who then became Count of Luxembourg. Charles had also been present at the battle of Crécy and had resolved not to waste his life. He was a hard-hearted, rational and calculating man, with a brilliant education from the University of Paris. He was determined not to become embroiled in any vainglorious or romantic wars in either Italy or Germany and to focus his energies where they served him best.

In 1348 Charles was crowned King of Bohemia. Charles then made Prague the capital of the Holy Roman Empire. To this day tourists flock to the Charles Bridge in that city, usually without realising that it is, in fact, named after this Count of Luxembourg. That same year the University of Prague, one of the most ancient in Europe, created two annual scholarships for Luxembourgish students.

A year later, in 1349, the Black Death struck Luxembourg, causing widespread death, suffering and fear. No one could explain the pestilence that was striking down one community after another. One rumour that began to circulate was that the Jews had poisoned the water supply. It simply didn't occur to the baying mobs that the Jews were dying of the disease as well and so the Jews were expelled from Luxembourg, despite some efforts by Charles to protect them.

In 1350, under Charles' reign, a certain Adelaide of Vianden married Othon of Nassau-Dillenbourg. The future implications of this match were enormous, linking Luxembourg's monarchy with that of the Netherlands in future centuries.

In 1353 Charles, being more concerned with his Bohemian kingdom than with Luxembourg, relinquished the heavily mortgaged territory to his half brother Wenzel or Wenceslas. Charles then proclaimed Luxembourg a Duchy in 1354 and continued to rule his empire from Prague.

Wenceslas ruled as the first Duke of Luxembourg and married Jeanne of Brabant and Limburg. He continued to rule Luxembourg from 1353 until 1383 and during his reign Luxembourg began to expand its territory in all directions, swallowing up land as far as Metz in present day France and the now Belgian and Dutch areas of Limburg. The earldom of Chiny was also attached to Luxembourg during this period. In terms of landmass the Duchy was about four times the size of present-day Luxembourg.

At the same time Luxembourg became loosely attached to the German kingdoms. Although the area was only loosely controlled by Luxembourg, the territory nominally under the Luxembourg crown was around 500 times the size of the present-day Grand Duchy.

In 1356 Wenceslas and Jeanne made Brussels their new capital. From here they ruled in some style surrounding themselves with luxuries and followers.

In 1367 Jews returned to Luxembourg following their expulsion in 1349. There was even a gate in the city known as *la Porte des Juifs*, the Jews' Gate. However their presence in Luxembourg was precarious and unwelcome.

In 1383 Wenceslas died and his nephew, Wenzel, became Wenceslas II, ruling from 1383 until 1388. In addition to his territory in Luxembourg Wenceslas was also Wenceslas the IV of Bohemia.

In 1384 an extensive circular wall was built around the impregnable Bourscheid castle, consolidating the position of its counts as a local force to be reckoned with. Indeed it was the Bourscheid dynasty who had played and were to play a very active role in the battles of Crécy, Agincourt and other French wars.

Wenceslas II, brother-in-law of Richard II of England, turned out to be a poor ruler and soon ran up considerable gambling debts. He used Luxembourg as a security for a loan and this soon fell into the hands of his creditors, plunging the land into civil war within a decade.

In 1391 the Jews were once again expelled from Luxembourg, this expulsion being motivated partly by superstitious fear over the return of the plague and partly out of a desire to wipe out debts incurred to moneylenders. Money lending was a profession that was forbidden to Christians and was one of the few allowed to Jews by law. This made them useful to corrupt and financially incontinent rulers like Wenceslas II. There was obviously little the Jews could do in the face of such betrayal.

In 1400 Mary of Vianden, an obscure Catholic saint, died. Her remains were buried at the parish church of Vianden where they remain to this day.

The castle of Vianden passed into the hands of the

Nassau family in 1417. It was the Nassau dynasty who became the royal family of both the Netherlands and Luxembourg a few hundred years later.

Between 1411 and 1461 the land was torn apart by civil war. This was waged by two factions, the House of Luxembourg, and a camp known as the *engagistes,* the latter group claiming that Wenceslas II had pledged the Duchy to them.

The last of the Luxembourg emperors was Sigismund who died in 1437. For the average inhabitant of Luxembourg the end of the imperial era came as a blessed relief from endless taxation and absentee rule. However it was this period of imperial rule that had forged the Luxembourgish nation and during which it created icons of its national identity such as castles, flags and dynasties.

Soon however the territory fell into the hands of Elizabeth of Goerlitz, one of the so-called *engagiste* and Wenceslas II's niece. In 1441 Elizabeth sold Luxembourg to Philippe the Good of Burgundy and in 1443 Burgundian armies stormed the fortifications of Luxembourg City in a surprise night time attack. Philip the Good of Burgundy paid off Elizabeth and kept the territory for himself. With the transaction now complete Luxembourg ceased to be a sovereign country and instead became a possession of a string of rulers and empires for many centuries to come. For the next hundred years Luxembourg remained a Burgundian possession, ruled from Brussels, and French was made the official language. Nevertheless Luxembourg managed to keep a sense of its former freedom alive in the language and attitude of its people. It is during this period that work began on the Burgundy Tower at the castle of Clervaux under Frederic de Brandenbourg. The work included new fortifications and a prison, illustrating the power retained by local counts.

In January 1467 Philip the Good died and was succeeded by his son, Charles the Bold. Charles the Bold's reign was marked by a constant struggle against Louis XI of France, despite Charles' own cultured French upbringing. Charles married Isabella of Bourbon and fathered a daughter, Marie of Burgundy. Marie took the throne in 1477, but her rule was marked by the disintegration of her father's achievements which had been shaky even during his lifetime. This process was accelerated by the relentless pressure of Louis XI of France who repeatedly attacked her lands. In a bid to find a protector she married Maximilian of Hapsburg in 1477. In 1482 Mary was killed when she fell off her horse and she was succeeded by her infant son Philip the Fair.

In 1478 rioting broke out and mobs attacked the Jews of Luxembourg who had filtered back following the 1391 expulsion. Their property was looted, their places of worship desecrated and young and old alike were beaten and tormented.

In 1479 the city fortress of Luxembourg was besieged by the French. This began a period of sustained violence during which the castle at Hespérange was destroyed in 1483. Nevertheless, it was during this period that a postal route was carved from Brussels to Vienna, crossing Luxembourg and leading to better communications for those with the means to travel.

Philip the Fair continued to rule until 1506 when he died of a mysterious disease. At this point Luxembourg passed into Austrian hands under the rule of Charles V of Ghent. Charles became ruler of Spain and then Holy

Roman Emperor in 1519, at which point he returned north. Charles V ruled for nearly half a century and it was during his reign the last of the Bourscheid dynasty died and their impressive fortress began to dilapidate from 1512 onwards.

In 1519 the ancient church of St Michael in Luxembourg City was rebuilt in gothic style. A church had existed on the site since 987.

In 1530 the Jews were once again expelled and this time the expulsion had a degree of finality. Jews would not return to Luxembourg until the arrival of Napoleon in the late eighteenth century.

Chapter Three: Luxembourg under Spanish, French, Austrian and German rule

From 1st until 10th September 1542 Luxembourg was briefly occupied by the French, following a siege of the city. They returned on 12th September 1543 and remained until 6th August 1544 when the Spanish laid siege to the otherwise impregnable fortress. During this period the ancient Altmunster Abbey was destroyed.

Despite the conflict however, the magnificent church at Hachiville was completed in 1544. The church became a place of pilgrimage and was renowned for its polychrome statues, depicting the story of the Virgin Mary.

Throughout this troubled period Charles ruled the area indirectly as Holy Roman Emperor but in 1545 the Spanish installed Pierre Duke of Mansfield as their governor. Mansfield remained governor of the city for nearly fifty years and was known to be a favourite of Charles. He was a rich and powerful man and in 1563 Mansfield began to build himself a fine residence in the village of Clausen, which he never finished. It was here that Pierre's son Ernest was born in 1580, though ironically Ernest went on to become a Protestant leader in the Thirty Years' War.

In 1554 a gunpowder explosion destroyed much of the city, and consequently there was a huge demand for new buildings.

In 1555 Philip II of Spain took control of the area and in 1558 Charles V, Philip's father, died, probably as a result of his lamentable diet. It is during this period of Spanish rule that many renaissance buildings were erected, including parts of the Place d'Armes and the oldest sections of the Grand Ducal Palace. Known as the *hotel de la Maison Royale*, the Grand Ducal palace was built in 1580 and included oriel windows and a long majestic balcony. Beyond the city, the castle of Hollenfels is mainly of renaissance construction.

From 1568 until 1609 war raged between Catholic Spain and her renegade Protestant province of Holland. Luxembourg however remained loyal to Spain under Philip II and was staunchly Catholic, the Reformation making very few inroads. Indeed Philip II was a firm advocate of the Inquisition, although he was accused of excesses in his private life and even of killing his own son. During the war Luxembourg became an important logistical centre for the Spanish forces as well as a religious and cultural centre. The Luxembourg Dominican Order at Ehnen dates from this era.

In 1589 Henry of Nassau, an ancestor of the ancient Dutch royal family, died and was buried at Vianden, the family's ancestral seat.

In 1593 the Duke of Mansfield acquired the castle of Beaufort, symbolically stepping into the shoes of earlier Luxembourgish counts.

In 1598 Mathias Birthon established Luxembourg's first printing press, a rather risky enterprise considering the proximity of the Inquisition and the religious authorities' paranoia regarding the printed word. Seven years later, Abbot Bertels of Echternach published the first history of Luxembourg.

Philip II died in 1598 and was succeeded by his daughter Isabella. Shortly after the start of Isabella's reign a Jesuit college was established in Luxembourg City around 1603, and located at the site of the Athénée. Within its first year nearly 200 students enrolled. The establishment of the college was vital in order to ensure a steady stream of priests in Luxembourg. However, it also brought the shadow of the Inquisition closer.

In addition to the college, two important abbeys were founded in Luxembourg City in 1606. These were the Abbey of Neumunster and the Abbey of St Jean.

It was under Isabella's reign that work began on the gothic cathedral around 1613, though at the time the cathedral was simply a large parish church. The church grew around an old Jesuit chapel, which existed on the site overlooking the Pétreusse valley and was built to plans by a monk from Mons known as Brother Jean du Blocq. Du Blocq worked under the direction of another monk, Brother Hoeymaker, a master church builder who had completed work on other great churches, such as those at the Belgian cities of Mons, Arras, and Tournai. The design of the new church had striking similarities with these Belgian churches and had many of Hoeymaker's hallmarks. In 1618 the church was completed. In its crypt was the tomb of John the Blind, who had been killed at the battle of Crécy in 1346.

In 1621 Isabella of Spain was replaced by her son Philip IV. In the same year, 1621, Philip de Lannoi, an ancestor of Franklin Roosevelt, left the castle of Clervaux and went to America. Back home the Lannois remained a powerful and prosperous famous family in Clervaux, contributing much to the growth of the town in later centuries.

In 1622 the fine baroque gallery of the nave of Luxembourg City's cathedral was completed by Daniel Muller. Such a style was in marked contrast to the simple and unadorned churches of the Netherlands. This illustrates the growing cultural and religious rift between the two countries, which had been close under the ministrations of St Willibrord and St Boniface in earlier centuries. Five years later the congregation of Notre Dame was founded in 1627, coinciding with the beginning of the cult of the Virgin Mary. The cathedral then became the focus of an annual pilgrimage on the fifth Sunday after Easter to venerate the Virgin Mary, who remains a very powerful and emotive symbol for many Luxembourgers to this day.

In 1630 some of the first Luxembourgers to cross to the New World joined the Dutch in New Amsterdam. These were the founders of a new Luxembourgish community in what was to become the United States.

In 1630 a monastery was founded at the northern town of Troisvierges. Such monasteries remained a powerful force in the devoutly Catholic land.

In 1631 the castle of Wiltz was remodelled. This marked the decline of the medieval feudal fortress towards a more residential Baroque chateau. However feudalism still remained in one form or other, and the counts continued to wield economic power.

During the Thirty Years War the French attacked Luxembourg, in 1635. These attacks resulted in famine and epidemics, and soon the French developed a reputation for ruthlessness. Most feared of all however, were the Croat and Polack mercenaries who took delight in raping and killing peasants. Once troops had devastated the fabric of village life or ruined a harvest by burning crops there was little the inhabitants could do but starve. There was little in the way of poor relief or stocks of grain to replace a lost harvest. In addition the killing of male peasants could deprive a family of its ability to farm the land effectively. The feudal nature of society also imposed the requirement to provide crops or money to the owners of the land. These problems did not in any way impede the construction of sumptuous Ansembourg Chateau in 1639 however.

The 1648 Peace of Westphalia brought a period of calm and growth to the country. This was the culmination of a lot of diplomacy designed to end the Thirty Years' War. The treaties that went up to make the Peace of Westphalia addressed disputes all over Europe but more importantly for Luxembourg, it ended the conflict between Spain and the Netherlands.

In 1653 a new and magnificent church was built at Troisvierges. It was adorned with priceless works by artists of the Flemish school. As was usual in European history most great art works were lavished on religious buildings.

In 1659 the Pyrenees Treaty, which ended the war between France and Spain, gave about a thousand kilometres of Luxembourgish land to France including the city of Thionville, where pockets of Letzebuergesch speakers remained until modern times. This is referred to as the first partition of Luxembourg. What was left of Luxembourg itself was to remain under Spanish rule with Philip IV still on the throne.

In 1666 the patron saint of the country was changed from St Quirin to the Virgin Mary, reflecting the staunchly Catholic ideology of the authorities.

In 1668 the 12th century castle of Brandenbourg was destroyed, reminding everyone that, treaty or no treaty, war was a constant factor in the life of Luxembourg.

In 1674 the Spanish built the *Casemates de la Pétreusse,* a honeycomb of tunnels and lookouts, improving the ability of the city to withstand siege if needed. Their precaution turned out to be justified.

In 1679 Louis XIV began a campaign to seize parts of Luxembourg, sensing weakness. During the incursions Louis XIV's army shelled and partially destroyed the iconic castle of Bourscheid. Then, in 1683, Charles II of Spain rather rashly declared war on France. This prompted France to renew its campaign in Luxembourg, during which the conquering French army deliberately destroyed two castles in Larochette in 1683. In 1684 Luxembourg City's fortifications finally fell to the French army, under the leadership of Marshal de Crequi, completing the conquest. Louis XIV was now at the apex of his power and his new conquest, along with the province of Alsace, was secured under the Treaty of Regensburg.

The French believed they had achieved their goal of '*réunion*' for Luxembourg. *Réunion* was a term devised by Louis XIV who, gorged with political power, felt he could revisit treaties and annex land that was loosely attached to territory granted to him under various treaties. A *Chambres de Réunion* or court was created to define the exact boundaries due to France, according to the French. Whilst this concept of reunion is groundless, Luxembourg did begin to fall more into the French cultural orbit during the seventeenth century, as is illustrated by the building of French style chateaux at Mersch and Ansembourg.

From 4th June 1684 until 28th January 1698 Luxembourg was under the rule of France and Louis XIV. The French engineer, Marshal le marquis de Vauban, added to the fortifications, to the extent that the city became virtually impregnable. Vauban had plenty of experience in this field, having been entrusted with the construction of a string of impressive forts along most of France's northern borders. In Luxembourg his works included the *Citadelle du St Esprit* which was completed in 1685, along with impressive the *Porte du Pfaffenthal*, a large fortified gate into the city. A convent needed to be demolished to make way for the fortifications, so Louis XIV ordered the *Hospice Civile* to be built on the other side of the river to house the displaced nuns. This was completed in 1684.

As a result of the formidable fortifications none of the neighbouring countries could safely allow an enemy power to control the city, which became known as the Gibraltar of the North. Its fortifications and its strategic location condemned Luxembourg to serve as a perpetual pawn for centuries to come. The French, however, destroyed the fortifications of the town of Esch-sur-Alzette for strategic reasons.

In 1687 Louis XIV arrived in Luxembourg in great style along with the heir apparent and a gaggle of followers which included the dramatist and royal biographer Racine.

However, ten years later, the 1697 Treaty of Rijswick obliged France to give Luxembourg back to the Spanish, and in January 1698 Luxembourg was restored to Spanish rule under Charles II of Spain. This was the second, albeit short, period of Spanish domination.

It is during this period of Spanish control that the church of St Jean and the *Hospice St Jean* were rebuilt. In later years these became the notorious Grund Prison which was used until 1980, with male prisoners being accommodated in the former church and women in the former hospice.

However in 1703 the French were back, resorting once

more to siege, and pursuing an aggressive and expansionist foreign policy. For them the Treaty of Rijswick had been nothing more than a humiliating truce, which they had no intention of honouring. Luxembourg remained under French control from 1703 until June 1713, when the Treaty of Utrecht and Rastatt transferred the Spanish Netherlands to Austria. The Treaty of Utrecht marked the end of Louis XIV's period of aggression. His country was drained by years of war and decadent court-life. From 7th January 1715 onwards the southern Netherlands including Luxembourg was ruled by the Austrian Hapsburgs, under the reign of Charles VI of Austria. During this time the country was relatively peaceful and prosperous. New economic activities included the growth of the tanning industry, which developed in Clevaux during the seventeenth century, by all accounts a smelly but lucrative business.

In 1723 a certain Father Raphael de Luxembourg arrived in the French colony of Louisiana, where he set up a cathedral in New Orleans on behalf of the French. Father Raphael is remembered for his work towards the equality of native Americans and Blacks and was one of several American-Luxembourgers who made a significant impact on American life.

In 1737 work was begun on the construction of the *Casemates du Bock,* a warren of tunnels and defensive caves hewn into the rocks of the old town. This complimented the *Casemates de la Pétreusse* built by the Spanish in the previous century, making the city ever more impregnable.

In the same year the pretty St Croix Chapel was completed overlooking the Moselle river at the town of Grevenmacher.

In 1739 the Chateau of Meysembourg was built, its

grandeur and opulence in marked contrast to the functional fortifications being built around the capital.

In 1740 Maria Theresa daughter of Charles VI ascended the Austrian throne upon her father's death. A lot of building work was carried out during this period of Austrian rule including work on the Ansembourg Chateau, which was rebuilt in baroque style with landscaped French gardens. One of the greatest achievements of the Baroque period was the construction of St Martin's Church at Bavigne in 1741. The following year the Church of the Congregation was completed in the Capital City. Then, in 1743, the Chamber of Deputies was built, originally as the town hall. In 1751 the present-day foreign ministry was completed, flanking the Cathedral. Perhaps the greatest baroque achievement of all however, was the sumptuous church at Koerich, which was completed in 1748 and topped with an onion-shaped spire.

In 1756 some of the worst recorded flooding in the history of the Luxembourg took place in the Alzette valley. As usual it was the peasants and the villagers who bore the brunt.

In 1761 a splendid *Orangery* was completed in Echternach, adorned with statues of the seasons. However the opulence of the new building underscored the different worlds in which the rich and the poor lived. Money was spent either on fine chateaux or on churches, for example the Loretto Chapel at Clervaux, built in 1762 to house the tombs of the lords of the town. A further example of lavish church building is the resplendent St Michael's Church at Mondorf, completed in 1766.

However, one source of employment was created for ordinary people with the opening of the Septfontaines pottery in 1767. By the end of the eighteenth century pottery and ceramic work had become an important industry in the country.

The Treaty of Versailles was signed in 1769 between Austria and France, fixing the borders between France and Luxembourg. One result of this was to cut the town of Mondorf into two. This remains the case to this day and one can cross the bridge to the French side and be back within less than a minute.

In 1773 the Jesuit College was forced to close under sustained pressure from opponents of the Catholic order. Jesuits were often seen as disloyal and treated with a great deal of suspicion and fear.

Luxembourg remained under Austrian control, with Maria Theresa at its head, until she was succeeded by Josef II in 1780. However Josef II's rule was clumsy and his leadership was to lead to trouble.

In 1789 a revolt broke out in the Belgian province of Brabant against reforms being carried out by Emperor Josef II. These were put down with some brutality and speed but a spirit of revolt was hanging over Europe, especially in France where a full scale Revolution broke out, followed by the march of France's revolutionary army across Europe.

Josef II died in 1790 and was succeeded by his brother Leopold II of Austria who was left with the unenviable task of restoring calm.

In 1792 the great German writer Goethe visited Luxembourg, staying at the riverside town of Grevenmacher. He was very taken with it, prompting him to write about it in his book *Campagne in Frankreich*. He also painted it and expressed a wish that the French painter Poussin had done the same, for only the French painter could do justice to the romantic and wild landscape. In addition to Goethe, Luxembourg attracted other romantic travellers with its thick forests, ravines and ruined craggy castles.

France invaded and annexed Luxembourg in 1792 and it was during this period, with the Grand Duchy under the control of the French Revolutionary forces, that feudalism was finally abolished.

Luxembourg was under French rule from 15th December 1792 until 28th April 1793 when it reverted to Austria under the rule of Francis II, the son of Leopold II. However, the French returned two years later in 1794. From 21st November 1794 until 7th June 1795 Luxembourg City was under siege for over seven months, making it the longest siege in its history.

Chapter Four: The Treaties of Versailles and London. The basis of statehood and the creation of a modern economy.

From 1795 Luxembourg was under the rule of the French Republic, a situation which was formalised under the Treaty of Campo Formio in 1797. The French began to apply revolutionary French law to the territory and in 1795 they abolished the court of feudal justice, which had been in place since the thirteenth century, completing the process of abolishing serfdom. In pursuit of their policy of radical secularisation, the French also expelled the friars at the Abbey of Echternach in 1795, ending a long history of scholarship and teaching. This policy was an anathema to many Luxembourgers.

The French were keen to tie their new possession into a web of empire-wide communications and immediately set about building new roads, and improving existing ones. However, the French Empire was stretched both financially and in terms of manpower. In 1798 Luxembourgers were drafted into the French army, sparking a revolt known as the *Kloeppelkrich* or war of the 'big clubs.' On receiving the news that they were to be conscripted, farmers in the Ardennes region armed themselves with clubs, pitchforks and axes to resist the French. The ring leaders of the revolt were soon arrested by the professional and well-armed French troops and taken before a tribunal. In order to de-escalate the situation, and perhaps out of pity, the judge offered to let the men off if they agreed to admit that they had not carried loaded weapons and that their aims had been misunderstood. They were offered the chance of clemency if they retracted from their protest. The men refused the French olive branch and about thirty five of them were either beheaded or shot. They defiantly repeated "we cannot lie" before being executed.

During this period of French rule Luxembourg was brought under the diocese of Metz and remained so until 1823. This was an unusual position to be in, as France was resolutely secular. This was of concern to many in staunchly Catholic Luxembourg. Indeed the issue of French secularism was a constant worry and was to remain so for decades to come.

In 1802 Boursheid Castle, one of the grandest of all Luxembourg's castles and a poignant reminder of a more glorious past, was finally abandoned and began to fall into disrepair.

In 1803 the French authorities introduced the so-called *franc germinal*, which became Luxembourg's legal currency.

In 1804 Napoleon became the leader of France and by extension Luxembourg. During the reign of Napoleon, the territory was one of the main sources of timber for the French war machine and became known as the *Departement des forets*, the Department of Forests. It is also during this period of French rule that the Jews returned after nearly 250 years. This occurred when a group of fifteen families settled in the Grand Duchy after moving from the French province of Lorraine. Within a decade there were seventy five Jews in Luxembourg and their status was assured by French decree in 1808.

In 1804 Napoleon himself visited Luxembourg and was granted the key to the city. He was given a salute of cannon fire accompanied by the peeling of bells. Napoleon, like most visitors, was impressed by the country and is said to have coveted deer from Clervaux which he wished to take back to his own chateau at Fontainebleau.

It was around this time that the now world famous Loosen family acquired vineyards in the Moselle region, beginning a long family tradition of producing world class wines.

In 1813 the *Eglise Protestante du Grand Duché,* the country's first official Protestant church, was opened. This move was made easier by the more laissez-faire attitude of the secular French occupiers towards non-conformist religion.

Following the collapse of France, Luxembourg was besieged by a coalition of anti-French troops and then found itself bounced from owner to owner. From 15th February until 9th March 1814 Luxembourg was under the district of the *Governement-général de la Belgique.* From March 1814 until 12th May 1815 it came under the jurisdiction of the *Governement-général du Rhin Moyen.*

At the Congress of Vienna in 1815, which was set up in order to sort out European boundaries following Napoleon's defeat, Luxembourg was on the agenda. Originally it had been the plan to tie Luxembourg into the German orbit. However King William I of the Netherlands was furious, seeing Luxembourg as his prize, and a compromise was reached whereby Luxembourg was made a Grand Duchy, a nominally sovereign state, although the monarch was William I of the Netherlands. The Grand Duchy was a crown possession of the Netherlands and William was its Grand Duke. For this reason civil servants were required to learn some Dutch. However Luxembourg was also to become a member of the German Confederation, the

Deutscher Bund. 26,000 Prussian troops were stationed in Luxembourg as a deterrent for a French invasion, under the leadership of General Friedrich Emil Kleist. Moreover, Luxembourg would have a number of seats in the German *Diet*, a parliament of 39 states, which included Denmark. The constitutional position was complex but apart from these provisos Luxembourg was deemed to be a sovereign state.

Under the Vienna Treaty, Prussia was granted over 2000 kilometres of Luxembourgish land in the second partition of Luxembourg. This included the town of Bitburg. Because of the treaty, the towns of Echternach, Grevenmacher and Vianden found themselves on the border, and some pockets of Letzebuergesch speakers were left inside Prussia, where they remained even as late as the 1930s.

In 1816 the first of a succession of devastating famines broke out. Once again peasants and villagers were left with little in the way of help and many had to leave their homes or die. The situation was aggravated by the behaviour of King William I, who was referred to as the 'Little Frog,' and who treated Luxembourg as a conquered territory, rather than recognising the limitations of a constitutional monarch.

In 1817 Grand Duke William I of the Netherlands instituted the creation of a 3000-man Luxembourgish militia. The men would sign up for five years, of which the first year would consist of active service and the rest of the time they would serve only three months a year as reservists. This was effectively the birth of the modern Luxembourgish armed forces, though the men were to serve under the Dutch flag. The Prussian garrison remained in place, with the historic *Church of the Congregation* being handed over for their sole use in 1817. This allowed the mainly Protestant soldiers a place to worship in their own language.

In the same year, 1817, work began on a new road connecting Luxembourg to the Belgian town of Marche, improving communication considerably by 1827.

From 1820 the castle of Vianden, historic seat of the Orange Nassau dynasty, had begun to fall into an alarming state of disrepair. Strange stories circulated about the ghosts of tormented medieval knights, playing dice with the Devil and trying to reclaim their souls. However, such decay merely added to the attraction for romantic travellers who continued to flock to Luxembourg. One famous visitor was the English painter William Turner who painted several water colours whilst in the country.

As part of the transfer of power from France to the Netherlands, Luxembourg was placed under the Belgian diocese of Namur in 1823. This came as a relief to those who feared integration with a secular France. In the same year, 1823, the first synagogue was built.

In 1830 Belgium erupted into open revolt against Dutch rule, inviting Leopold of Saxe-Coburg to become its king. Luxembourg on the whole backed the revolt, following William I's misrule and the outbreak of famine. On 16th October 1830 the provisional Belgian government declared that Luxembourg was an integral part of Belgium. The political situation was confused and hampered by poor communication. To add fuel to an already tense situation a further famine broke out in 1831. Unfortunately the explosive political situation put paid to a plan to connect the rivers Maas and Rhine and in the event only one and half miles of the canal was tunnelled out near the village of Hoffelt before being abandoned.

On 15th November 1831 the Netherlands and Belgium hammered out a deal dividing Limburg and Luxembourg between the two countries. Not surprisingly Luxembourg refused to recognise the agreement but for the next nine years Luxembourg was administered by Belgium anyway. Luxembourgish deputies attended the Belgian Congress and Prussian troops guarded Luxembourg City on behalf of the Dutch crown, Luxembourg's militia having been suspended during the period of Belgian rule. This arrangement lasted from 22nd October 1832 until 19th January 1839. Luxembourg's limited sovereignty, gained in 1815, was effectively suspended.

Despite the constitutional flux, work on the town hall was completed in 1838.

Eventually, at the Treaty of London in 1839, the Western powers recognised Belgium as a sovereign state. William I of the Netherlands was obliged to recognise this fait accompli of Belgian independence but the treaty was bad news for Luxembourg as it ceded the western French speaking provinces of Luxembourg to the new Belgian state, including much of the Ardennes. Moreover, the treaty was unpopular in Belgium as well, where many were angered at the loss of the remaining part of Luxembourg. The third partition represented an enormous territorial loss for Luxembourg, with two thirds of its remaining territory and half its population now included in Belgium. A small pocket of Luxembourgish speakers remains to this day on the Belgian side of the border, referred to by Luxembourgers as the Areler Land. In the Grand Duchy only 175,000 citizens remained on a territory of 2586 square miles.

In turn Luxembourg was granted autonomy under the Treaty and was declared a Grand Duchy on 19th June 1839, with the Grand Duke giving his formal agreement to the partitioning of Luxembourg. Thus William of the Netherlands became once again the monarch of Luxembourg. The Grand Duchy's political institutions were strengthened and they began to mature into a functioning state, with state functionaries being given the choice of using the French or German languages. It quickly became more fashionable and common to use French however.

The Luxembourg militia, an embryonic army, was reinstated and included an infantry battalion based in Echternach, a cavalry division located in Diekirch and a small artillery company in Ettelbruck.

One effect of the new constitutional arrangements was the abolition of the death penalty, in practice if not in theory. Although prisoners no longer suffered the death penalty from this time on, death remained the prescribed punishment for five offences until the 1970s. These were murder, attempt on the life of the sovereign, successful attempt on the life of the heir to the throne, arson with fatality, and causing explosion with fatality. Exceptionally, the death penalty was used in 1946 to punish nine collaborators and traitors and was formally abolished for all crimes in 1979.

Luxembourg's Jewish community became more settled with the constitution issues resolved and in 1838 the *Consistoire Israelite*, the Jewish consistory, was established. Until then all matters relating to community affairs and religious law had been referred to the Jewish community of Trier in Prussia. A further step towards establishing an independent Luxembourgish religious life was taken in 1840 with the creation of the Vicariate Apostolic of Luxembourg and the ordination of the first Vicar Apostolic, J.T Laurent.

In 1840 William I of the Netherlands abdicated and William II became the King of the Netherlands and Grand Duke of Luxembourg as part of the Orange-Nassau dynasty.

Drawing the Grand Duchy further into the German orbit, Luxembourg joined the Prussian customs union, the *Zollverein* in 1842, enjoying strong economic growth as a result. As part of the *Zollverein*, Luxembourg began using the Prussian currency known as the *Thaler*.

Despite economic growth, there were famines in 1840 and then again in 1846-7, driving local farmers to emigrate.

One success story of the 1840s however, was the opening of the Bofferding Brewery by Jean Baptiste Bofferding. Bofferding grew to become one of the country's best known companies.

The process of mass emigration to the United States began as a steady trickle as far back as the seventeenth century but it gathered pace in the mid 1840s, spurred on by the growth of the American rail system and the opening up of the American Mid-West. A further wave of emigration occurred from 1846 until 1860 when Luxembourgers were tempted across the Atlantic by cheap farm land.

By the 1850s Luxembourgers were beginning to have positions of influence in all areas of American life.

Chicago in particular became popular with Luxembourgers and by the 1850s the city even boasted its own Luxembourg Club. It is now believed that there are more people of Luxembourgish descent in Chicago than there are in Luxembourg City and more American-Luxembourgers than inhabitants in the Grand Duchy.

However it was not all bad news back home in the Grand Duchy. Deposits of iron ore were discovered in the *Minette* region of the country. This coincided with a new method of removing phosphorous during smelting, revolutionising steel production in the Grand Duchy. In addition, it was discovered that the waste from the smelting made ideal fertiliser, perfectly suited to the soil in the north of the country. Because of the industrialisation of the Esch-sur-Alzette region, tens of thousands of immigrants began to arrive in Luxembourg, mostly from France and Italy. The pace of this immigration was such that by the beginning of the twentieth century 47% of the Grand Duchy's workforce was foreign. At the same time emigration from the Grand Duchy began to slow.

On 26th July 1843 a new law was passed, making French the language of education in primary schools, and replacing German. However, German remained the popular language of everyday communication for most working class Luxembourgers.

In the same year the status of 'town' was awarded to Luxembourg City, Diekirch, Echternach, Grevenmacher, Remich, Witlz and Vianden.

On 12th December 1843 William I, the former king of the Netherlands and Grand Duke of Luxembourg, died three years after his abdication. He was not widely mourned.

In 1844 a small groups of Mennonites arrived in the Grand Duchy, named after their founder, a sixteenth century Dutch Anabaptist called Menno Simons. They established some small farms near Echternach where they lived and worked quietly.

In the same year work began on the large church at Mersch.

In 1845 a state-funded seminary opened in the capital enabling Luxembourgish priests to be trained and ordained at home thus filling a void left by the closure of the Jesuit College in 1773.

In 1846 the cavalry and artillery divisions of the militia were scrapped and replaced by a single infantry unit based in Echternach and Diekirch. It was believed this could improve efficiency.

It was during 1847 that a first Letzebuergesch dictionary was published, compiled by J.F Gangler. It was an important first step on the road to official recognition of the tongue.

During 1848 a major revolt erupted in France and the French government was eventually overthrown and replaced by Louis Napoleon Bonaparte, who was related to the Dutch royal family. Taking heed of the events in France, King William II of the Netherlands and Grand Duke of Luxembourg granted Luxembourg a new and liberal constitution in 1848. He hoped thus to defuse any tensions and prevent insurrection in the long-term.

From 1st August 1848 until the start of December Gaspar-Theodore-Ignace de la Fontaine served as leader of the government. On 2nd December 1848 Jean-Jacques Madelaine Willmar became the government's leader.

In the same year, the grandfather of Luxembourgish periodicals, the *Luxemburger Wort* appeared for the first time. It was, and remains, a conservative and authoritative publication.

Following the death of William II in March 1849, William III became king of the Netherlands and Grand Duke of Luxembourg. In the long run he did not turn out to be a popular king, nor was he an absentee ruler, building himself a chateau at Birtringen near Colmarberg. The castle was surrounded by lavish grounds and was built in an English-Gothic style, underlying the foreign nature of the ruling dynasty. In addition to the work at Birtringen, the castle of Vianden was restored and so remains one of the greatest feudal castles in Europe.

In 1850 William's brother, Prince Henry of the Netherlands, took up residence in the Grand Duchy, building a chateau for himself in the village of Walferdange, where he stayed until 1879.

In 1852 the first postal stamps were introduced.

On 23rd September 1853 Mathias Simons became Prime Minister, replacing Jean-Jacques Madelaine Willmar.

In 1855 Jean Pierre Pescatore bequeathed a substantial collection of paintings and other works of art to the city of Luxembourg, forming the basis of the present-day museum. Pescatore was the son of a Luxembourgisch banker and tobacconist, and was born in 1793. However at the age of 37 he set himself up in Paris where he made his fortune and began collecting art. The museum grew to become the country's foremost art collection.

1856 saw the creation of the *Banque Intérnationale à Luxembourg,* which was authorised to print Prussian *Thaler* banknotes.

Problems at home were exacerbated in 1856 when the conservative and reactionary Dutch king, William III, imposed a constitution on Luxembourg, overriding the 1848 constitution which had been introduced by his father. The new constitution strengthened the power of the Grand Duke, and by definition the power of the Dutch king. However, rather than snuff out national feeling, William III's imperious and arrogant attitude strengthened it.

In 1859 the first railway was opened, operated by a company known as the *Prince Guillaume Railway*. This had required a huge feat of engineering. Viaducts and tunnels were built, allowing tracks to be laid through the county's rocky and hilly terrain. This included the most famous railway bridge in the country, the Viaduct or *Passerelle,* which was completed in 1861. The first link was with the French city of Thionville, in 1859 and the following year the system was linked to the Belgian city of Arlon. The arrival of the rail system was a great step forward for the Grand Duchy, enabling the transportation of steel products and coal to and from the south and also enabling more mobility of population.

In 1859, when the first railway opened, Antoine Zeum composed Luxembourg's national anthem, entitled *de Feierwon*. The last verse contained the traditional slogan of national assertion, *mir welle bleive wat mir sin* or 'we wish to remain what we are.' That year, building work on the *Chambre des Députés* was completed, to house the Luxembourgish parliament.

Between 1862 and 1870 Luxembourg became host to one of France's most illustrious writers when Victor Hugo sought refuge in the Grand Duchy, staying mainly at Vianden. Hugo, who was already in his late fifties, enjoyed his time in Luxembourg, attracted by the wildness of the landscape. During his time in Vianden, Hugo rose at dawn to write but in the afternoon he relished walks in the Petit Suisse region with its waterfalls and craggs. Like other romantic writers he enjoyed the thrill of gothic horror engendered by the ruined hilltop castles and thick pine forests.

However, it seems that Hugo may not have been too lonely, enjoying the company of a young Juliette Drouet during his stay. Drouet was the widow of a Communist and Hugo found that she provoked him to think. For this reason, and perhaps others besides, he arranged for her to reside at a house opposite his own. It seems Hugo fitted in well with the townsfolk of Vianden who sought his advice on restoring the castle and, on more than one occasion, the local band serenaded him. Hugo is even said to have helped put out a fire, mucking in with the local volunteers. He also enjoyed the more genteel life at the town of Mondorf, and he spent time at the pretty riverside village of Schengen, from where he travelled along the Moselle. Hugo had been elected to the French parliament in 1850 as democrat republican but following a coup in 1851 he was forced to flee to Brussels and then later to the Channel Islands. He returned to France in 1870 but he paid homage to his host town of Vianden in the work *L'Année Terrible*.

During the same period another writer, Michel Rodange, was active in Luxembourg. Rodange wrote *The Adventures of Renard* (The fox). It was a caricature of the political landscape in the Grand Duchy and he remains one of Luxembourg's most regarded writers. Rodange died in 1876 and is commemorated by a statue in the Place

Guillaume at the heart of Luxembourg City. Another artist active in the mid-nineteenth century was Jean-Baptiste Fresez who edited a work known as the *Album Pittoreque*, containing pictures of the Grand Duchy.

By the middle of the nineteenth century significant iron ore deposits were being successfully exploited, making the country richer and therefore more sought after by her neighbours. Iron ore strengthened Luxembourg's industrial base, adding a new branch to the more established steel production, along with some limited mining.

On 26th September 1860 Baron Victor de Tornaco, son of a long-established aristocratic family, became Prime Minister.

The following year, 1861, work was begun to restore the Romanesque Abbey at Echternach. The restoration, completed in 1868, was controversial and some felt too rigid and classical.

In 1861 a Luxembourgish pastry chef, Nicolas Namur returned home from California. Namur had left Luxembourg at the age of 20. Having learned the skills of patisserie in Metz and then Paris he crossed the Atlantic in 1854. It was there that he opened his first shop. On his return to Luxembourg, Namur opened a café in 1863, in rue des Mamer. The café went from strength to strength and by 1870 the premises had moved to rue des Charbons. Namur became and remains to this day a Luxembourg institution. It is to Luxembourg what Betty's is to Yorkshire. It became a centre of social life and the 'grand dames' of Luxembourg society would come to eat cakes and to see and be seen having their afternoon *klatsch*.

1862 saw the opening of a new narrow-gauge rail link connecting the towns of Remich and Mondorf to the capital. The two towns developed as tourist destinations and the rail link allowed greater access to the German and French borders. Mondorf in particular began to take off as a place for patients to 'take the waters.' This arose when a certain Maitre Ledure had noticed that the water in a German spa town was similar to that of Mondorf. The salt content of the water was believed to cure a whole host of conditions.

In July 1862 a railway line opened between the capital and the town of Ettelbruck, providing a boon for the sleepy provincial town.

Continued famine, debt and other hardship began to drive an increasing number of Luxembourgers overseas once again, especially to the United States. Luxembourgers settled in the farming areas of Minnesota, Ohio, Wisconsin, Iowa and Nebraska, often joining those who had emigrated in the 1840s. Families left *en bloc* and many other families joined them to set up Luxembourgish communities in the new land. As more and more immigrants settled the process became easier, with networks flourishing to cater for the new arrivals. Many of the immigrants used the Red Star Line from Antwerp to cross the ocean, often in horrific conditions. As a result of exploitation, the Luxembourgish government passed a law in March 1870, requiring the regulation of emigration agencies. This had the desired result of putting many of the disreputable companies out of business, and a small group of the larger agencies flourished. Foremost amongst these was *Derulle-Wigreux & Sohn* who arranged passage for thousands of Luxembourgers. Soon Luxembourgish villages were flourishing in the United States complete with Luxembourgish schools and churches. Many institutions were created in the United

States to meet the needs of Luxembourger-Amercians. This included the *Luxembourg Benevolent Society* in 1870, and was followed by the *Luxembourger Sick Benefit* in 1871. In 1887, the *Luxembourg Brotherhood* began life as a fraternal insurance company on Chicago's South Side. Then, the *Luxembourg Gazette* became the first Luxembourgish publication in the United States. The periodical, under the leadership of Nicholas Gonner and his son, published news stories from the old country as well as news of Luxembourgish communities in the United States.

In the 1860s the German Confederation began to fracture. This was potentially dangerous for Luxembourg, being in constitutional limbo, with a Dutch king as her head of state but with Prussian troops on her soil. In addition Luxembourg's economy was linked to the German Confederation through the *Zollverein* or customs union. One exception to the customs union was alcohol with the result that goods and people were checked by customs officers. With the partitioning of Luxembourg some thirty years previously, the country was now far too small to ever be self-sufficient.

In 1864 the *Association typographique*, or printers union, became the country's first trade union.

In 1866 the railway was extended from Ettelbruck to the town of Troisvierges in the north of the country and an extension rail link was opened from Troisvierges to the Belgian border in February 1867. This linked the Grand Duchy to a wider European rail network, enabling travellers to make better connections to the Belgian ports. Two years later, a partly Belgian-run company created the *Prince Henri Railway*, running trains from Grevenmacher to Esch, via Diekirch and Noerdrange.

In 1867 the Abbey of Neumunster was rebuilt in its present form, later becoming the notorious Grund Prison.

In a move of unparalleled cheek, King William III of the Netherlands offered to sell Luxembourg to Napoleon III of France in March 1867. Napoleon III was keen to use Luxembourg as a buffer against Prussian influence in the east and a price of 5million florins was agreed. Needless to say William's subjects were not consulted on this proposed sale of their land. Prussian leaders however were furious and threatened to declare war, despite a French invitation for Prussia to agree to the purchase amicably. Prussia was not about to have Luxembourg, an integral part of the German economy as well as a hugely strategic piece of real estate, given over to the arch enemy.

Eventually Prussia agreed to a conference on the issue, more as a public relations exercise than a real negotiation. On 11th May 1867 the second Treaty of London reaffirmed Luxembourg's status as a state, building on the autonomy achieved by the Treaty of Vienna in 1839. Prussia agreed to withdraw a garrison of Prussian 7000 troops and reaffirm Luxembourg's neutrality. At least that way, reasoned the Prussians, the French wouldn't get Luxembourg either.

Luxembourgers danced in the streets as the Prussians left. However the Prussian troops left one small legacy in the remnants of a tiny Lutheran community. They also left a small Prussian cemetery in the rue Jules Wilhelm which remains to this day.

The Prussian troops were replaced by units of Luxembourg's tiny militia in September 1867. In the same month a new regiment, the *Corps des Chasseurs*, was created with over 1500 men. However, part of the London agreement was strict demilitarisation and as a result Luxembourg could not provide any real military deterrent beyond this tiny force. She therefore pinned her security on treaties and the goodwill of Europe's big players. As an act of good faith Luxembourg destroyed many of her ancient fortifications which had for so long been fought over by her neighbours. However not all the fortifications could be destroyed without risking the collapse of the city into the valley below, and the work took nearly twenty years. In their place a park was built by Edouard André, offering spectacular views over the valley. André designed a similar park in Europe's other micro-state, Monaco.

On 3rd December 1867 Lambert Joseph Emanuel Servais became Prime Minister, replacing Baron de Tornaco.

In 1868 the *Luxemburger Zeitung* was first published. In contrast to the conservative *Luxemburger Wort*, its main rival, the *Luxemburger Zeitung* was more liberal, and even radical in its editorial stance.

In May 1868 the size of the militia was limited to 500 men, Luxembourg being naturally wary of antagonising her neighbours or of being accused of breaking the conditions of her neutrality.

On 17th October 1868 the liberal constitution, which had been first introduced in 1848, was restored. The constitution stated simply:

The Grand Duchy of Luxembourg forms a free state, independent, and indivisible.

One welcome legal development was that primary education was made compulsory. The new constitution also introduced state funding for all recognised churches in the Grand Duchy. Religious independence from foreign states was accomplished in 1870 when Luxembourg finally became a diocese, with its own Bishop. Thus the Notre Dame church became a cathedral. However the diocese was only recognised by the Luxembourgish state three years later in 1873, when the Bishop was obliged to swear allegiance to the crown.

Following France's defeat in the Franco-Prussian War in 1871, Prussia assumed control of the *Prince Guillaume Railway*. This was to have serious ramifications for Luxembourg, as it would give Prussia, and later Germany, a reason to interfere in Luxembourg's affairs. In 1872 Prussia signed an international convention in which she undertook not to use the *Prince Guillaume Line* for military purposes.

In 1874 former Prime Minister Mathias Simons passed away and on 26th December 1874 Felix de Blochausen became Prime Minister. In 1875 former Prime Minister Baron de Tornaco died.

In 1875 a census took place, recording the population of the Grand Duchy at 205,156 of whom 5,895 were foreign.

In 1877 Nicholas Muller became the first American Luxembourger to be elected to the American House of Representatives. This illustrated a certain coming of age for the American Luxembourgish community.

In 1878 a law was passed adding the French words "*les bains*" to the name of the town of Mondorf. By now Mondorf was becoming quite a fashionable resort town and the addition of the French tag underlined the increasing cultural leaning towards France. The hot springs and mineral properties of the water began attracting a cosmopolitan following, with many patients coming to seek cures from rheumatic, nervous and bronchial disorders. Large hotels and sanatoriums were built to cater for such patients and a range of other facilities were established to keep them amused, including parks and restaurants.

In 1879 Luxembourg adopted the Belgian legal code, making only a few modifications. The Belgian legal code was quite close to the French Napoleonic Code and the system was considered effective and compatible. The Luxembourgish state was too young and too small to have a totally unique system of common law and had not been able to build up a complete body of statute law in the short years of its independence.

The famous photographer Edward Steichen was born in 1879. Within months his family emigrated to the United States. Steichen would become one of Luxembourg's most famous sons.

The so-called Bessemer process for the production of steel from pig iron had been developed in Britain in 1856 and in 1884 these new methods were introduced to Luxembourg, enabling the Grand Duchy to become a major steel producer. The town of Esch-sur-Alzette grew into a 'steel metropolis' during this time with many open-air mines scaring the landscape and chimneys bellowing soot into the air, becoming a Luxembourgish equivalent of England's dark, satanic mills.

Mining also began in the village of Walferdange where large deposits of plasterstone were discovered. By around 1880 a system of railway tracks was built into the tunnels which grew to around 16km. In later years archaeologists discovered that this plaster stone had been used in nearby Roman villas.

In May 1881 the militia system was finally abolished and along with it the *corps des chasseurs* regiment. This was replaced by a more formal and structured Luxembourgish army consisting of a regiment of 170 volunteers and 125 'gendarmes,' a kind of militarised police. The law allowed for this force to be increased to 250 in times of crisis. A military band was also created.

In 1883 the last of Luxembourg's ancient fortifications were pulled down to comply with international treaties. As a result, Prussia relented her stand on the construction of a rail link to French town of Longwy, allowing engineers to begin work. The whole affair illustrates the complex tightrope that Luxembourg, a sovereign state, had to tread, caught between two suspicious and hawkish neighbours but with no means of defending herself.

In 1884 a statue to King William II of the Netherlands and Grand Duke of Luxembourg was erected in the Place Guillaume, built by a French artist. This again underscored the peculiarity of the Grand Duchy with a foreign monarch honoured in a capital city where most street names are in French.

On 20th February 1885 Jules Georges Edourd Thilges was elected Prime Minister, replacing Felix de Blochausen. He was in turn replaced by Paul Eyschen on 22nd September 1888. Eyschen was to remain Prime Minister until his death in 1915.

In 1885 the famous composer Franz Liszt arrived in Luxembourg. Liszt was visiting his friend Michael Munkacsy, a Hungarian painter who had a mansion at Colpach in the west of the Grand Duchy. Michael Munkacsy lived in some grandeur but he had had a deeply unhappy childhood which marked him for life. As a young man he had made his way to Vienna and Munich, later gaining fame for his religiously themed paintings. His work was even hung in the Hungarian parliament. Having made it financially, he bought himself a grand villa in Paris and also proved himself to be very generous to other artists, remembering his own trials and tribulations. In 1874 he purchased the chateau at Colpach to use as a summer residence for himself and his wife. He befriended compatriot Liszt, the two men having a mutual interest in religion. After visiting the German musical centre of Bayreuth Liszt decided to come to Luxembourg and visit Munkacsy. However Liszt was dying. He had been diagnosed with dropsy earlier that year and was weak. Liszt was able to give a performance to the Musical Society of Luxembourg, playing *Liebestraum*. However, this turned out to be his last performance and he died of pneumonia on 31st July that year. Munkacsy died fourteen years later after becoming morbid and being admitted to a mental hospital at Endenich.

In 1886 the Grand Duke took over patronship of the thermal baths at Mondorf Les Bains. This gave the resort a certain cachet and added to its growing prestige abroad.

In 1889 Nicholas Gonner, an American Luxembourger published the book *Die Luxemburger in der Neuen Welt*, a detailed account of the emigration story.

Chapter Five: The fin de siècle, and the Great War

In 1890 there was a split in the line of succession of the House of Nassau when the last male descendent of Orange Nassau line, Willem III, died and the Luxembourgish crown passed to the Nassau-Weilburg branch on 23rd November 1890. As a result the Luxembourgish and Dutch thrones divided and Luxembourg achieved its own royal line, with the Grand Duke Adolf of Nassau Weilburg becoming the first truly Luxembourgish Grand Duke.

In 1890 the former Prime Minister Lambert Joseph Emmanuel Servais died.

A year later, in 1891, work began on enlarging the 16th century Grand Ducal palace.

Towards the end of the nineteenth century a system of tramways was opened, linking the station with the old town, crossing over the Viaduct, a spectacular bridge that spanned the Pétreuse valley. The steam powered trams then followed the Boulevard du Viaduct, now known as the Boulevard Roosevelt before turning up rue Athénée and swinging east along rue Notre Dame and then north up rue du Fosse. From here they ran down the centre of the Grand rue and up avenue de la Porte Neuve where they terminated. The creation of a tram network revolutionised public transport in the city and facilitated a fast connection to the railway station which would otherwise have been too far to be convenient. The location of the station on the south of the city created a second pole of commercial activity with new shops and restaurants springing up to cater for travellers along the avenue de la Gare, taking advantage of roomier premises outside the confines of the old town.

In 1892 the Pescatore Foundation was created to provide housing for the elderly in the west of the city. Traditionally the elderly had been accommodated by their families, and the need to build special sheltered accommodation was indicative of growing social and economic mobility. As the younger generations emigrated, the elderly were often left behind.

In Echternach, the famous *Denzelt*, an old court building dating back to 1539, was remodelled in 1892. As in Victorian England there was a growing tendency to 'improve' historic buildings.

In 1894 the Luxembourgish artist Joseph Kutter was born. In future years Kutter went on to become one of the Grand Duchy's most famous artists.

1894 saw the opening of a new synagogue in the capital to meet the needs of a community that by now consisted of over 150 families. Many of these families had set up their own businesses and had become an integral part of the economy. Five years later, in 1899, a second synagogue was opened in the town of Esch-sur-Alzette.

In 1897 a large neo-gothic style church was completed in Dudelange, a small town near the border with France. St Martin's Church became the third largest church in the country and was finished with Byzantine-style murals. This was in keeping with a Byzantine revival in Catholic church building in other parts of Europe and is a forerunner of London's magnificent Westminster Cathedral, which was furbished in 1899.

In 1899 a 12.5 meter memorial to Luxembourgish heroes was built at Clervaux, indicative of a feeling of rising patriotism. The heroes had died fighting the French attempt at introducing conscription in 1795.

In 1900 a small community of Seventh Day Adventists was established for the first time, showing increasing religious pluralism.

During the same year, but on the other side of the Atlantic, Edward Steichen, the photographer, became an American citizen at the age of 21. Steichen was already passionate about photography and had met with professional success despite his young age. He was commissioned to photograph celebrities such as Richard Strauss, Matisse, Greta Garbo, Gary Cooper and even Winston Churchill. In 1902 he helped to create the *American Photo Secession Group*.

In addition to Steichen's photography, another artistic development was to flourish at the turn of the century. This development began as a result of events over the border in France. Following the ceding of Alsace-Lorraine to the Prussians in 1871, the former regional capital of Nancy was suddenly sundered from its hinterland. The town became destination for a large number of refugees and *émigrés* from the now Prussian parts of the former French region. By 1900 Nancy had become an artistic centre, producing high class ceramics and furniture, and the town buzzed with creative spirit and from the energy created by the arrival of new artists from the east. Cabinet makers, glass workers and architects converged on Nancy from places such as Metz and Strasbourg, keen to escape the suffocating atmosphere of Prussian occupation. The so-called *école de Nancy* or the Nancy School was born and its ripples began to filter over the border into Luxembourg.

Art Nouveau itself was a fairly revolutionary movement. It was radical and broke sharply with stuffy established values in art and architecture. It is no coincidence that it flourished in areas far removed from established cultural centres and capitals. Provincial cities such as Nancy, with a confident growing cultural and economic scene, were ideal hothouses for the new style, the new centres keen to assert an alternative sense of identity from their capitals. Thus Art Nouveau grew in Brussels as well as Darmstadt, Barcelona, Glasgow, Munich and even Chicago. For Luxembourg there had always been a need to assert independence from the powerful neighbouring nations of France and Germany.

Also influencing the Grand Duchy was Brussels, which was closely connected to Luxembourg through economic union as well as the recent rail links. Brussels was an almost schizophrenic city divided between French and Dutch speakers and overshadowed politically by Paris. A taste for the exotic had arisen in Brussels following the Belgian experiences in Africa and a flourishing Art Nouveau style arose under the influence of King Leopold II, producing great architects and artist such as Victor Horta and Henry van de Velde.

As Art Nouveau architecture tended to cluster in cities that were growing at the time when Art Nouveau was flourishing, Luxembourg was ready to espouse the new style. This was especially the case for Mondorf les Bains which had recently been given a rail link, Grand Ducal patronage and a host of new facilities. Architects built villas in the new style which was the height of modernity and artistic fashion. The new homes boasted extravagant doorways of curved concrete and flowery glass panels along with exuberant coloured ceramic tiles. Staircases were graceful and spiralling, and floors were covered with exquisite mosaics. The style flourished in

Luxembourg City too, notably in the Bourbon area, where street upon street of stylish new apartment buildings were built. New shops were opened with Art Nouveau features, such as the Rosenthal department store, and other shops along the exclusive Grand rue. Art Nouveau architecture also blossomed in the industrial city of Esch-sur-Alzette, with fine examples of the style being concentrated on the rue Alzette.

However Art Nouveau was not the only style prevalent in the turn of the century building boom. Luxembourg had inherited a solid Germanic style of architecture during the latter part of the nineteenth century, with its fair share of the so-called *Rundbogen Stil*, a solid Romanesque style of building with hallmark round windows. Many new buildings were erected during the later nineteenth century, especially in the area around the railway station on the south side of the Pétreusse valley. Yet another prevailing influence, evident in the extension of the city towards the station, is that of the Hausmann style, imported from France, where long wide boulevards fanned out from the station area.

In 1900 a small grocery shop was opened in Luxembourg City by Joseph Leesch. Seventy years later Leech's family would go on to found the country's foremost food shopping chain, *Cactus*.

Some reforms were made to the country's heath system at the turn of the century. In 1901 work was completed on Luxembourg's only mental asylum, at the town of Ettelbruck, and during the same year a contributory sickness insurance system was introduced. Most hospitals continued to be staffed by nuns.

The following year new health and safety regulations

were imposed by the government, forcing mining companies to improve safety and working conditions for miners.

In 1903 the *Pont Adolphe* bridge was completed by the French engineer Séjourné, linking the so-called *Oberstadt* or old town with the new development on the station side of the city. The bridge, which soon became known as the *nei-breck* or 'new bridge', complemented the existing *Viaduct,* which had been the only link to the Bourbon plateau until then. The style of the new bridge was solid and conservative, with a huge inward facing bow and a series of arches. On the station side of the bridge was the German-style *Caisse d'Epargne,* with turrets reminiscent of a Teutonic hunting lodge. Building on the new side of town was rapid and usually homogenous in style, intersected by wide streets and avenues, and lined by new saplings and iron street furniture.

The fin de siècle produced a host of inward tensions and national self-questioning of which architecture was only one symptom. Many Luxembourgers had difficulty in finding a cultural home, the country being too small to furnish much of one from within. The conflict centred on the use of language and French became the language of the high-brow.

Outsiders too, found the Luxembourgers hard to define as a nation. The 1897 *Baedeker Guide* summed them up as follows:

The inhabitants, though of pure Teutonic race, are strongly French in their sympathies, especially in the upper classes. The popular language is a low-German dialect, very unintelligible to strangers; the official languages are French and German.

In 1904 former Prime Minister Jules George Edoard Thilges died.

In the same year, the *Prince Henri* railway was finally extended to provide a link with the town of Pétange on the French border, and with easy access to the large French town of Longwy. Longwy was a major industrial centre and good links with Luxembourg's industrial *Minette* region were vital for the economy.

The following year, in 1905, Adolph's son William IV became Grand Duke, a cause for national celebration and pride.

In 1906 Esch-sur-Alzette officially became Luxembourg's second city. This was merely official recognition, as the city had been in a state of rapid growth for over half a century. The population of Esch continued to grow, and that year the *Bourse de travail* or labour exchange was created, facilitating the movement of workers in the country, and thus better managing the flow.

A mausoleum was built over the grave of St Willibrord in the crypt of the abbey at Echternach in 1906.

In the same year, the *Union des Syndicats Chrétiens* or Association of Christian Unions was founded. This body of Christian groups worked together to improve welfare.

In 1907 the *Palais Municipal* was completed in the capital city. In the same year, the famous *American Building* was completed at the corner of rue Saint Philippe and rue Notre Dame. This building, bedecked by a huge American eagle, would serve as an emigration agency and travel agency.

That year 'town' status was granted to Ettelbruck, Differdange, and Rumeldange, reflecting the growth of those localities over the previous fifty years.

In 1908 Marie Anne, the grand daughter of Adolph and wife of Grand Duke William IV, became the Grand Duchess Regent. However in 1912 Marie Anne was replaced by her daughter Marie Adelaide as Grand Duchess.

In June 1910 an aviation festival was held at the town of Mondorf-les-Bains. This was the cause of great excitement, both at home and abroad. Massive biplanes took to the skies and circled the town to the delight and fascination of the crowds below.

In 1910 a modern Romanesque church was built at Clervaux, to the design of a Dutch architect, and inspired by the famous monastery at Cluny in France. This complimented the Benedictine abbey of Ss Maurice and Maur, built the year before. A small Anglican church was opened in the capital city in the same year, catering for the tiny resident English community, in addition to the growing number of travellers.

In 1911 the fledgling steel firm ARBED, which stands for *Acièries-Réunies de Burbach-Eich-Dudelange*, was created under the leadership of Emile Mayrisch. ARBED rapidly grew into one of the Grand Duchy's principal firms, employing a huge workforce and producing a significant slice of the nation's GNP. A huge building was built at the station-end of the town to house the new company's headquarters.

In the same year, a system of compulsory pension contributions was introduced. This would go some way to easing poverty amongst the elderly but it would take years before its benefits were felt.

In 1912 the Luxembourgish language, Letzebuergesch, was introduced in the national school curriculum for the first time and in 1914 the education minister Nicholas Welter set the first standards for spelling of the language, although this was not official. It would take the persecution of the Second World War to see the Luxembourgish language metamorphosise from a dialect into a formal language.

In 1914 the Luxembourgish Red Cross was formed, as was the football club, the Red Lions.

It had been clear for a number of years that an epic conflict was looming in Europe. However Luxembourg had always been at pains to avoid becoming embroiled in any alliances, preferring to maintain a policy of strict neutrality. Indeed it was required to do so by the international treaties which secured her independence. It came as something of a shock therefore when on Saturday 1st August, the bridges over the Moselle and Sure rivers were sealed.

The event caused alarm, and Luxembourg demanded from France and Germany that they formally reconfirm Luxembourg's neutrality. France responded by promising that both Belgium and Luxembourg's neutrality would be respected. Worryingly Germany failed to respond.

Shortly after the sealing of the bridges, two German officers and men of the Prussian Trier Regiment arrived at the railway station in the small Luxembourgish town of Troisvierges, in the north of the country. One of the officers then demanded control of the telegraph posts and, to the confusion of the Luxembourgish authorities, the soldiers proceeded to rip up about 100 meters of track. The Prime Minister telegraphed Berlin to try to discover what was going on. The German foreign minister responded by saying there must have been a misunderstanding and that Germany would respect Luxembourgish neutrality according to the 1870 agreement, *provided France did the same*. There then followed reports that the bridges had been reopened.

However on Sunday 2nd August 1914 German troops crossed the river at Remich and Wasserbillig. Using the railway network, which had been under German control since the end of the Franco-Prussian War in 1870, the well-prepared German forces used armed trains to move troops towards the south of the country and the capital. Station officials were warned to expect a 'special train from Trier' in the early hours of the morning. They were not told it would be an armoured troop train, however. Luxembourg was unable to offer any resistance, its armed forces consisting of a royal ceremonial guard. Writer Francis Gribble summed the situation up when he wrote:

Luxembourg could no more withstand a Prussian army than a kitten could hold a staircase against a pack of hounds

By 5am the invasion of Luxembourg was more or less complete. The German government then threatened Belgium, demanding that they allow German troops to cross her territory, in exchange for a promise that Belgian sovereignty would be upheld. Luxembourg was made no such offer.

Shocked, the Luxembourgish government objected vigorously, both to the German Imperial representative in the Grand Duchy, as well as by telegram to the German foreign ministry in Berlin. In addition the Grand Duchess personally telegraphed the Kaiser in protest.

An urban myth has arisen to the effect that as the first German troops moved into the capital, the Grand Duchess and the Prime Minister Paul Eyschen stood on the Adolphe Bridge to meet the invading army, led by General

Tessmar. The pair remonstrated with the General who apparently ignored them. This cannot be proved, however a more likely story is that a police van was parked in the middle of the bridge to impede the invaders. The officials and police who attempted to protest or who got in the way were dismissed at gunpoint. At 10.00am an emergency proclamation was issued appealing for calm.

That Sunday, there was a scramble to leave the country. British and French tourists sought to get home, along with foreign workers. Some managed to get onto trains bound for Belgium but some would remain trapped in Luxembourg for the duration of the war, or else were interned in Germany. One such British tourist was Francis Gribble, who was trapped at his hotel in Vianden. Gribble describes his experiences in his book *In Luxemburg in War Time* which was published in 1916.

At 5pm on the day of the invasion a cable was sent to the Prime Minister Paul Eyschen in which the Imperial German government apologised for the invasion, an event it claimed was necessary to protect its military and railway interests. The later had some degree of plausibility as most of the Luxembourgish rail network was under German control. In addition France had a poor track record of staying out of Luxembourg when it suited her. The cable promised to reimburse the Luxembourgish state for any damage caused by the German actions.

French troops were soon involved in a fire fight with the Germans at the border post of Petit-Croix that day, during which two German cavalry officers were killed.

On 3rd August a further German cable set out to clarify the nature of the invasion which, according to the Germans, was to be 'temporary', and during which the rights of all

Luxembourgers would be respected. Luxembourgers were also assured of the 'impeccable and disciplined' behaviour of the German troops. Once again France was accused of being the first to compromise the Grand Duchy's neutrality thus forcing Germany's hand. Luxembourg dismissed this claim out of hand. The Germans however cited some dubious evidence of 650 French troops on bikes entering the Grand Duchy, a charge which was strenuously denied by Luxembourg.

During the night of 4th August the German 4th Army and VIII Army Corp, under Von Wurttemberg, moved into Belgium as part of the *Schlieffen Plan*. Belgium had refused to bow to German demands and put up a gallant fight to slow the attack.

On 4th August Chancellor Bethmann-Hollweg of Germany formally justified and clarified his country's actions by accusing the French of massing troops on Luxembourg's borders in the days prior to the invasion. The German government promised to withdraw their troops as soon as possible and recognised that their actions may be unjust but were necessary. In response the Luxembourgish government forcefully made the argument that Luxembourg was a neutral country which had been occupied when not at war. This fact, they believed, made the legal situation different, especially in terms of how the civilian population was to be treated and in the light of the Hague Convention on the rights and duties of occupied territories in war.

However, up to 3200 able-bodied Luxembourgish men had managed to leave the country before the invasion, and during the course of the war most of them volunteered for service in the French army. Over the course of the war nearly 2800 were killed, representing a huge per capita sacrifice.

From 14th August until 25th August the German forces pushed the French 3rd and 4th armies away from Luxembourg's borders and back inside France. However, as the German 4th Army marched onwards into France and Belgium, they left behind a garrison to secure the capital, and the railways. The Germans also deployed *Landwehr* troops, a paramilitary unit of semi-uniformed men, roughly equivalent to Britain's territorial army. In this way they could free up more troops to fight the French. However Luxembourg remained an important command post.

In order to secure the capital, the Germans pulled down the trees that lined the avenues. They claimed this would enable them to use their machine guns if required and give them a clearer line of vision. In the countryside orchards were uprooted and bunkers and gun emplacements were dug, causing hardship to local farmers.

The occupiers were already aware of likely trouble makers and made a series of 'preventative arrests.' This indicates that the German secret service had been active in Luxembourg for some time before the invasion. The prisoners were taken to Trier and many were later released and kept under surveillance.

For the rest of the war the Grand Duchy remained occupied and was used as a logistical support base for the German army. The city of Esch-sur-Alzette became the headquarters of the General and Crown Prince Wilhelm von Hohenzollern. As such, the city became one giant military hospital and logistical base, serving Germany's Western Front, and the city's factories were closed. This was due in part to the break in supply from France, from where much of the raw materials required in steel making came from. Instead, Luxembourgish workers were put to work for the German war effort, causing great resentment. The occupiers also set up a recruitment station in an effort to persuade Luxembourgers to join the army but with very little success.

Despite its neutrality, Luxembourg was kept under martial law, with its citizens being subject to restrictions on travel, censorship, and rationing. The authorities were obsessed with spies, a fear that resulted in regular stops and searches of civilians. This in turn caused resentment. During the course of the occupation some Luxembourgers were executed for spying, although the authorities usually took the precaution of removing the prisoner to Germany first, mindful of the anger such executions might cause.

Parliament however was allowed to function as normal, on condition that no action was taken contrary to German interests. Indeed five different prime ministers represented the country during the occupation, illustrating the continuity of a relatively unfettered political scene.

In March 1915 the question of whether Germany had had cause to invade the Grand Duchy blew up again, following a German inquiry into the issue. This could hardly be considered an impartial inquiry and was more of a transparent public relations exercise which caused much anger and resentment in Luxembourg. The report intimated that the Luxembourgish government had tacitly agreed to the occupation, an accusation which added insult to injury for the Grand Duchy.

Even today some questions remain as to why Germany felt it necessary to invade Luxembourg at all. For example was there any credible evidence to suggest that France was prepared to use Luxembourg to strike at Germany first? France obviously had its own interests to consider and bearing in mind that France had no qualms in conquering swathes of North Africa, it is doubtful that she would put Luxembourg's right to neutrality ahead of her own security. However, the most likely explanation is that Luxembourg was quite simply in the way. Germany needed to sweep into Belgium in order to get at France's undefended northern border. Whilst it may have been possible to bypass Luxembourg and follow the same attack lines it was simply not necessary. Luxembourg was not able to fight back and not invading it would have impeded the invasion of Belgium. The delay would have given the French more time to prepare. In addition, there was no guarantee that, once the northern front had been opened along the Belgian border, the French would not attack through Luxembourg had it been left alone by Germany. There does not seem to have been much ideological motivation for the invasion or much evidence of German atrocities beyond the blatant rape of Luxembourg's sovereignty, some forced labour, some isolated executions, and restrictions on movement. Nevertheless in a study entitled *Germany's Aims in the First World War* Professor Fritz Fischer does put forward the argument that the Kaiser and his cohorts had deliberately set out to subdue Belgium as a vassal state, and to annex Luxembourg. This is backed up by comments made by General Bronsort von Schellendorf who vowed to annex swathes of northern Europe, including Luxembourg. However, Luxembourg was not annexed and for the duration of the war no serious measures were taken to do so.

One curious side-effect of the occupation was the

huge increase in church attendance. This was both a form of national assertion and a source of comfort to many.

The war was never far away. The guns in France and Belgium could often be heard, and wounded soldiers were a regular sight at the railway stations. This prompted a few Luxembourgish nurses to volunteer for service in military hospitals.

In October 1915 the veteran leader Paul Eyschen died. From 12th October until 6th November 1915 Mathias Mongenast was the acting prime minister. On 6th November 1915 Herbert Loutsch of the *Chreschtlech-Sozial Vollekspartei,* the CSV, became Prime Minister and served until 24th February 1916. The CSV was and is the Christian Social People's Party representing 'Christian social policies.'

In March 1916 the *Letzeburger Arbechter-Verband,* a united trade union congress, was founded. This indicates a certain *laissez-faire* attitude by the German occupiers, though such an event would never have been allowed under the Nazi occupation of 1940.

Victor Thorn of the *Demokratescher Partei*, the DP, took over as Prime Minister until June 1917. The Democrats and the CSV continue to be the mainstream parties in Luxembourgish politics to this day.

Grand Duchess Adelaide stayed in Luxembourg throughout the occupation. She was a young and beautiful woman and yet she remained unpopular with her subjects, being somewhat aloof. Adelaide loved court life and she wanted nothing less than a Luxembourgish aristocracy to fawn on her. This was quite simply alien to the down to earth Luxembourgers. Adelaide therefore looked to Prussia for inspiration and there were rumours that she may marry a Prussian prince. Such a move would certainly have suited the occupiers. In the event such a marriage did not take place but her subjects remained wary nonetheless.

In 1917 the *Luxembourg Brotherhood* in the United States began lobbying President Woodrow Wilson to come to the Grand Duchy's aid and join the war. Eventually the United States did join the war, during which photographer Edward Steichen served in the American forces as commander of the photographic division of the US navy.

On 19th June 1917 Léon Kauffman was elected prime minister.

During April 1918 around 500 Austrian troops were stationed in the Grand Duchy. Their job was to build a railway branch line from Oetrange to Berchem using Italian POWs. This prompted a furious response from the Luxembourgish government to the Austro-Hungarian authorities, accusing them of joining Germany in the invasion of the Grand Duchy's neutrality. Austria apologised and explained that the troops were under German command and reiterated the promises of 1914 to make good any damage. The fact that Luxembourg could and did protest, underlines the comparatively passive nature of the occupation.

On 28th September 1918 Emile Reuter replaced Léon Kauffman as Prime Minister.

On 6th November, a few days before the armistice General Tessmar, the German commander, issued a statement announcing an immediate German withdrawal from the country. On 18th November, a week after the armistice, General "Black Jack" Pershing of the United States declared Luxembourg liberated and on 22nd November French and American troops entered the Grand Duchy.

Chapter Six: From one war to the next 1918-1939

Following the end of the war Luxembourg withdrew from the *Zollverein,* the customs union with German, with effect from 1st January 1919. It was unthinkable for the economic union to continue, both for patriotic as well as practical reasons. In the meantime the Belgian Franc was to be used, although a Grand Ducal decree introduced for the first time the term 'Luxembourg Franc.' Belgian currency had already been a recognised form of legal currency prior to the war, with the German Mark being legal tender alongside it, so it was relatively easy to manage this transition.

Two clauses were inserted into the Treaty of Versailles with regard to Luxembourg. Articles 40 and 41 ended all German influence in Luxembourg and obliged Germany to honour any future arrangements made by the Allies regarding the Grand Duchy.

As soon as German troops had cleared Luxembourg questions were raised about the behaviour of Grand Duchess Adelaide, whose cosy attitude towards the occupier did not go unnoticed. She was not alone in this and other members of the government came under scrutiny. The allied powers also viewed her with suspicion and on 9th January 1919 Parliament met to debate the very future of the monarchy. Outside angry crowds gathered and clashed with the French troops who were called upon to disperse them. For some of the protestors it must have felt that one occupying force had been replaced with another. Within a matter of days the Grand Duchess was forced to step down in favour of her sister Charlotte, who assumed the throne on 15th January, aged 23, thus beginning a reign that was to last until 1964. Just days before, Grand Duchess Princess Charlotte had married Prince Felix of Bourbon Parma.

Almost immediately Charlotte began the task of healing her Grand Duchy but, learning from the mistakes of the past, she carefully avoided becoming embroiled in political wrangling. In this way she concentrated on overcoming the negativity which existed towards the royal family.

It was during this period that Luxembourg introduced a system of basic social security. This was long overdue, with many Luxembourgers living in conditions of squalor and hardship.

In the United States, the *Luxemburger Gazette* closed down, following accusations of a pro-German bias in the years up to, and during, the Great War.

As the dust settled, Belgium believed it could reinvent itself as an enlarged state and European power, not only by annexing some of Germany's territory but also by incorporating the Grand Duchy. Thankfully for Luxembourg this concept of *la Grande Belgique* or Greater Belgium was rejected at the Paris Peace Conference.

In 1919 Luxembourg-born Robert Schuman, the future architect of the EU, was elected as a Deputy to the French parliament, serving as a moderate conservative. This came about as Schuman had been living in the region of Lorraine, which had been annexed by France at the end of the war, automatically conferring French citizenship on him and his family. Schuman was born in Luxembourg however, in 1886, to Luxembourgish-speaking parents. He later went on to become a leading member of the French government and a pioneer of the EEC.

On May 15th 1919 Parliament took the step of amending the constitution, limiting the powers of the Grand Duke. The amendment did allow for the Grand Duke to veto any parliamentary legislation but no monarch has ever done so. The constitution was also amended to allow female suffrage for the first time.

On 28th September a referendum was held in which Luxembourgers voted to retain the monarchy rather than become a republic. 66,885 voted to keep the monarchy against nearly 17,000 who voted against. The royalist camp was helped by popular Catholic sentiment opposed to the anti-clericalism prevalent in neighbouring France. There were fears that a republic could be a step towards annexation by France, a not unrealistic fear given France's track record and the presence of French troops.

Nevertheless, in a further referendum Luxembourgers chose to make France their primary economic partner. However France lost interest in the plan and Luxembourg was forced to go with second best, which was an economic pact with Belgium. The economic union, signed on 2nd July 1921 with Belgium, was less advantageous than a union with France could have been. Known as the *Belgian Luxembourg Economic Union*, the pact in fact proved disastrous for Luxembourg's economy, which no longer had free and open access to Germany. The economic union came into effect on 1st May 1922 despite reservations.

During the early 20th century there was a steady stream of migration away from the countryside, partly due to a sluggish agricultural economy and partly due to an increased emphasis on steel production. This led to an increase in the size of the main towns, especially Luxembourg City and Esch-sur-Alzette. It also led to some overcrowding and social problems. One problem was that, once removed from tight-knit communities, people felt less constrained by ties of mutual respect. After all, in a village it was vital to behave or else face exclusion. In a city that need lessened.

Yet despite this migration into the centres of industrial production, the economy continued to suffer a post-war slump, and in 1919 the blast furnaces at Rumelange were closed, indicative of poor economic health. In 1920 miners and steelworkers formed the *Syndicat des Ouvriers Mineurs et Métallurgists,* a new trade union. Industrial relations were beginning to sour. The same year the government introduced a maximum 8-hour day but social conditions continued to deteriorate, and in 1921 Luxembourg saw its first ever general strike. In order to alleviate some of the economic misery, the government took the step of introducing a limited system of unemployment relief in 1921.

On January 5th 1921 Jean, the first son of Grand Duchess Charlotte, was born. This was followed on January 24th 1924 by the death of the former Grand Duchess Marie Adelaide. She had gone into exile tainted by accusations of collaboration with the Germans and was just 29 at the time of her death.

In August 1922 the first International Commercial Fair was held in the Limpertsberg area of the city, drawing hundreds of stall holders. It was a welcome boost of economic confidence, and became an annual event.

1924 saw the moving of the now famous *Namur* café to the prestigious main thoroughfare, the Grande rue. By now George Namur, the son of its founder Nicolas Namur, had taken over the reigns of the business. The café was a glittering, smart meeting point for upper class women, bedecked in feather hats and fur coats.

The Grand rue also became the focus of the new modern Bauhaus style of building that had begun in Germany as part of the architectural expressionist movement. The new buildings that sprang up at various points were pure white, streamlined and flat rooved, in sharp contrast to the gothic renaissance and *Rundbogen* style of buildings around them.

The two railway companies that ran the Grand Duchy's rail network were brought under the joint control of the Belgian and Luxembourgish governments in May 1924. This move was considered necessary in order to provide a more efficient service, as well as to fill the void left by the removal of German control in 1918. Luxembourg's small size meant it was difficult to run the network in isolation.

On 19th March 1925 Pierre Prum was elected Prime Minister only to be replaced on 16th July 1926 by Joseph Bech of the DP. Joseph Beck later served as the foreign minister in exile during the Second World War.

In 1926 the *Viticulture Research Station* was opened in the town of Remich, and was dedicated to improving the quality of Luxembourg's famous Moselle wine. Luxembourg's wine producers had benefited from the 1920 economic union with Belgium, as Belgium's own wine industry had collapsed in the early part of the century and Luxembourgish producers could enjoy duty-free access to the Belgian market. Moreover, Luxembourgish growers had been innovating with their products and the *Caves St Martin* vineyard in Remich had introduced sparkling Moselle wine for the first time a few years earlier.

A few kilometres to the south of Remich at Mondorf,

state architect Paul Wigreux completed a new pavilion at the spa, making the resort a by-word for modernity and chic.

In 1926, paid holidays were introduced for workers for the first time in the country's history.

Across the Atlantic, the Luxembourgish community in the United States numbered around 50,000 by the 1920s, and in 1926 the *Luxembourg News of America* began publication in Chicago.

Back home, the steel company ARBED was going from strength to strength and was employing over 60,000 workers, many of them from abroad. Indeed the 1926 census recorded that one in four inhabitants of Esch-sur-Alzette was foreign, the majority of whom were either German or Italian. Under the leadership of Emile Mayrisch, ARBED forged links with Germany and France and contributed to post-war reconstruction, with a formal international agreement on steel being signed in 1926. Mayrisch became famous for his philanthropy, creating schools in the forests for disadvantaged children as well as turning his villa in the town of Dudelange into a sanatorium for children with TB. His castle in Colpach became something of a centre for literature and art, with artists and politicians enjoying the hospitality of his wife Aline de Saint-Hubert. The castle seemed to attract art. Mayerich had bought the castle in 1917 and this had originally been the home of Hungarian artist Michael Munkacsy. It was here that Munkacsy had entertained composer Franz Liszt during his last year alive.

However on 5th March 1928 Emile Mayrisch was killed in a car accident. Within a few years his carefully built international agreement with France and Germany had collapsed. None the less, in the years before the Second World War Luxembourg ranked seventh in the league of world steel producers.

In 1924 a young artist named Joseph Kutter arrived back home in the Grand Duchy, after 30 years in Munich where he had grown up. Kutter had been heavily influenced by the German expressionists. However on his return to Luxembourg he was not successful in getting his art across to the public, despite winning the prestigious *Prix Grand-Duc Adolphe* for his work. Kutter and his artist friends Klopp, Schaak, Tremont, Cito and Rabinger eventually left the *Luxembourg Artistic Circle*, feeling frustrated at the lack of appreciation amongst their compatriots.

During the twenties improved communication allowed for a growth in the country's tourist industry. The country was now on an international rail route and offered romantic scenery and ruined castles, as well as relatively modern facilities. In Clervaux the famous castle dating back to the 15th century was transformed into a hotel catering for Belgian, British, German and Dutch tourists, in 1927. Two years later, in 1929, restoration work was undertaken on the ancient castle at Hollenfels. This was vital to preserve one of the country's greatest monuments.

On 1st January 1928 Luxembourg's stock exchange or *bourse* came into being, less than two years before the Wall Street Crash.

In 1929, the first steps were taken towards the creation of a national radio company, although it would take a few more years before broadcasting would begin.

1929 saw the opening of the country's first Jehovah's Witness' congregation in the country. This added to the growing number of non-conformist denominations represented in the overwhelmingly Catholic country.

The Luxembourgish economy was not in a strong position during the late twenties and a further economic blow was dealt by the Wall Street Crash in 1929 which saw currency devaluation and the closure of many steel plants. Luxembourg depended on France for its iron ore and on Germany as a market for its steel. Both countries were now in difficulty and, as a tiny country, Luxembourg could not hope to avoid being dragged down with them. The response of the government to the recession was to liberalise banking laws in order to attract foreign investment. The government was especially keen to attract those holding companies, eager to avoid taxation elsewhere.

Another step in reducing economic hardship was the creation of the *Service des logements populaires* in 1929. This government-backed agency offered cheap loans, enabling workers to buy their own homes.

In 1930 Joseph Kutter, the Luxembourgish expressionist artist, began to enjoy his first international success, with his work being shown at exhibitions in Munich, Paris and Brussels.

As Luxembourg developed into a modern, industrial state with an increasing flow of population into the towns, it became clear that the old police structure was no longer effective. In 1930 the police forces were centralised to form a single force, although the armed *gendarmerie* remained a distinct force. Prior to the centralisation police forces had been communal.

In 1930 the famed *Poll-Fabaire* wine cellars were established in the town of Wormeldange, renowned for their sparkling wine.

However, there was a black cloud on the horizon

and, in March 1933, a small group of German nationals living in the Grand Duchy set up a local branch of the NSDAP, the Nazi party abroad. This consisted of secret cells in league with the Nazi party in Germany and was only open to citizens of the Reich. Luxembourgers could not join. Hitler was extremely wary of foreign collaborators. He viewed those who acted against the interests of their own people with contempt, but he regarded those who acted in their nation's best interests as dangerous.

In 1931 the French census revealed that over 21,000 Luxembourgers were resident in France. In Luxembourg too, there were large numbers of foreigners, notably a significant group of German citizens and their descendants. Many of these were involved in farming or in commercial activity, and many were married to Luxembourgers. The 1935 census noted a total of 258,544 Luxembourgers and 38,369 foreigners.

On July 19th 1932 Luxembourg, Belgium and the Netherlands signed the Ouchy Convention, agreeing to a partial reduction in trade barriers between their states. This was to culminate in the Benelux Economic Union in 1960, almost thirty years later.

In December 1933 Radio Luxembourg began broadcasting from a huge transmitter at Junglinster, three years after the company's creation. It proved very popular with audiences all over Europe, especially in the United Kingdom, where an outraged BBC and Post Office tried to have it banned. British newspapers even refused to advertise its schedule. One source of British wroth was the use of frequencies which were deemed to break international convention. Luxembourg waved such objections aside however, and Radio Luxembourg grew from strength to strength.

During the 1930s many art deco alterations were made to the cathedral in Luxembourg City, including the nave. There were also Art Deco shop fronts built in the town of Esch-sur-Alzette, along with some hotel lobbies in the capital. It was during this period that the *Grand Hotel Alfa* was opened, catering for visiting dignitaries and even royalty. Luxembourg's other foremost hotel, the *Grand Hotel Cravat*, was also catering for the rich and famous in sumptuous surroundings.

At the other end of the market, Luxembourg's first youth hostel opened its doors in the border town of Steinfort in 1933, offering cheap, clean and basic accommodation to young hikers and cyclists from all over Europe. The following year the *Ligue Nationale Luxembourgeoise pour les Auberges de la Jeunesse* or Luxembourg Youth Hostel Association was founded.

In 1934 expressionist painter Joseph Kutter met the critic Joseph Emile-Muller. Muller sang the praises of Kutter's work, notably its realism and two years later the Luxembourgish government commissioned two of his works, both views of Luxembourg, which were then displayed at the Luxembourgish Pavilion at the Paris Exposition. This was Kutter's big break.

Another budding artist of the time was Jean Noerdinger, a Luxembourger from Diekirch, who had emigrated to Chicago in 1925. Noerdinger had broken ranks with the *Luxemburger Kunstverein,* the Luxembourgish artists' union and arbiter of fashion and taste, when he introduced modern elements. Noerdinger participated in the 1933-34 *Century of Progress Exhibition.*

In 1935 many of the country's steel mills were forced to close their furnaces in the face of growing international recession. In the absence of any social security or sources of alternative employment this caused much hardship for those affected.

In 1936 Albert Kreins, an 18 year old Luxembourger, formed the *Luxemburger Volksjugend,* modelled on the Hitler Youth. Initially Kreins had tried to join the Hitler Youth but had not been allowed to do so, on account of his citizenship. Despite this, he was a guest of the Hitler Youth leadership at the 1936 Nuremberg Rally. It was on his return from the rally that he set up the *Luxemburger Volksjugend* in September 1936. The LVJ, as it was known, adopted a white rune with a black shield as its emblem and attracted approximately thirty members.

During the same year the *Luxemburger National Partei* was founded, based on hard core fascist ideology. Despite the fuss its creation caused, it did not prove popular with Luxembourgers. Fascism, or indeed any form of political extremism, did not sit well with Luxembourgers. As a small country with no recent imperial past or grand conquests there was little in the way of past glories to refer back to. Nor was there much internal discord or established history of racism to build on in this relatively harmonious nation. Moreover, Luxembourg remained a staunchly Catholic country for whom secular fascism and the cult of a human leader was quite alien.

During the mid to late 1930s the government undertook a spate of public work projects. For example, in 1936 Bourscheid castle was declared a national treasure and some basic renovations were carried out. Then in 1937 the airfield at Findel was opened, although it remained little more than a strip of grass with a hanger. In the same year the river Sure was dammed above the small town of Esch-sur-Sure, creating an important power reservoir but at the same time drowning the valley of Bavigne. Nevertheless the reservoir contributed significantly to the nation's self-sufficiency. This project was followed by the building of a new railway terminal in Luxembourg City, which was undertaken between 1936 and 1938.

On 5th November 1937 Prime Minister Pierre Dupong was elected, representing the CSV. He was to remain Prime Minister throughout the war and led the government in exile.

War felt imminent by 1937 and few Luxembourgers were under any illusions that their tiny Duchy would escape unscathed should the conflict break out. During the mid to late 1930s Luxembourg's Jewish population was swollen by over 3000 refugees from the Third Reich, who joined the original Jewish population of just over 1100. In addition, about 300 Jews fled Luxembourg for the United States, sensing great danger ahead. The Jewish community had become well-established in the Grand Duchy, with synagogues in both Luxembourg City and Esch-sur-Alzette. There were also Jewish communities in Ettelbruck, Differdange, Grevenmacher, Mondorf and Remich, as well as a tiny Jewish agricultural settlement in Medernach.

Despite the clouds of war, Luxembourg celebrated the centenary of its independence on 19th April 1939. With an eye on Germany's annexation of other territories, Luxembourg's tiny army was boosted by an additional 300 men in February 1939, the first time the government had ever taken advantage of a law allowing for an increase in the armed forces since their creation in 1881.

On 22nd April Parliament listened as a long list of the nation's achievements was read out and Luxembourg declared its intention of remaining a sovereign state.

As the summer wore on, tension rose. Yet only days before the outbreak of war both the German and French governments reassured Luxembourg that they would respect her neutrality, in an echo of 1914. It cut little ice.

On 29th August Parliament granted full emergency powers to the Grand Duchess and her cabinet.

On 6th September Luxembourg formally and publicly reiterated its neutrality, again citing the 1907 Hague Convention. To this end all acts which could be viewed as antagonistic to any foreign state were outlawed. Nevertheless Luxembourgers were outraged at German actions and were vocal in their criticism. This in turn led to a rising tide of outrage in the German state-controlled press at this perceived lack of moral neutrality.

As early as 1938 the government had begun installing a long series of defences along both its French and German borders and now zig zag barricades and barbed wire were erected on bridges and roads were narrowed. Other bridges were covered in concrete blocks, allowing only pedestrian access. All flights over Luxembourgish territory were outlawed on 2nd September 1939, which did not stop flights by both the French and German airforces however. In addition, deserters from both German and French forces were interned. Although Luxembourg was scrupulously going through the motions of impartiality it was clear who the real foe was. However there remained the possibility that France could attack first in a pre-emptive strike on Germany through Luxembourg, an eventuality the Grand

Duchy was keen to prevent.

Economic controls on imports and exports were rushed through in conjunction with Belgium in order to prepare for the coming conflict. There remained a hope that the country might escape occupation in the same way that the Netherlands had remained neutral in 1914. However in such an event the Luxembourgish economy risked a dire situation, due to its economic dependence on both France and Germany.

The commander of the Grand Duchy's small army was Major Emile Speller and by 1940 the army consisted of thirteen officers, 255 gendarmes and 425 soldiers. In the short time left before hostilities began, Speller adopted a strategy of minimising damage and allowing time for those who needed, to escape. To this end he ordered the evacuation of villages on the German border. On April 3rd plans were drawn up for the evacuation of Luxembourg City. Around 50,000 residents living near the Maginot Line on the French border were eventually evacuated into France.

After the war, secret documents were released showing the orders that Adolf Hitler had made in regard to the invasion of Luxembourg. These orders go some way to disproving the argument of a long-term premeditated war plan regarding the Grand Duchy. In fact Hitler's earlier orders make it clear that Luxembourg's neutrality must be respected. However, by October of 1939, with Germany and France now officially at war, Hitler began to plan for the invasion. For the time being, an uneasy truce reigned, referred to by the Germans as the *Sitzkrieg* or 'sitting war.' On 9th October 1939 Hitler issued orders that troops be massed along Germany's borders with Belgium and Luxembourg, but that such moves be camouflaged as defensive troop movements. Just over a week later, on 18th October, Hitler authorised the invasion of the Grand Duchy but forbade the use of air strikes, in order to minimise civilian deaths. This caveat points to a possible feeling of kinship that Hitler may have had towards Luxembourg. In any case the plans for "Offensive Yellow," the pre-emptive strike on the Low Countries were set in motion. Time was running out for Luxembourg.

Chapter Seven: 'mir welle bleive wat mir sin' Luxembourg under the jackboot

On the evening of 9th May the German authorities issued a communiqué, in which they accused France of plotting an attack on Germany in collusion with the Low Countries. Therefore German military forces would need to 'safeguard the neutrality of these countries.' The German authorities instructed the Luxembourgish government to prevent its population resisting the imminent invasion which was 'forced' on Germany in order to prevent French aggression. Germany nevertheless promised to respect Luxembourg's independence. The communiqué was something of a mystery. At first glance it seems to negate the concept of *Blitzkrieg* or lightning surprise attack. However the time given was a matter of hours, just enough time for the Luxembourgish authorities to instruct their troops not to fight and to get civilians out of the way. Germany and France were already at war and the French were as ready as they could be. Moreover just because Germany intended to march into Luxembourg was not necessarily a direct threat to the Allies who had already appeased Hitler on several occasions.

Alerted by this communiqué and reports of German troop movements along the Moselle river, the royal family fled to France, along with hundreds of refugees, arriving in Paris four days later on May 13th.

On Friday 10th May 1940 Germany launched their lightning attack on the Grand Duchy, Belgium and France. For Luxembourg the attack came around 4.30 on the morning of the 10th as motorised columns of the *German*

Army Group A smashed their way into the country. Neither the tiny army nor the country's 250 police officers resisted, in order to save lives. In the event only one militia man and seven police were wounded.

At seven in the morning the leader of the German delegation to Luxembourg took himself to the seat of the Luxembourgish government and declared that the Reich had taken Luxembourg 'under its protection.' Luxembourg was placed under martial law. Due to the flight of the royal family to France, Luxembourg was deemed to have sided with the allies and thus Luxembourg was considered 'an enemy state under occupation.'

Later that morning French troops crossed into the south of the country and engaged German forces there, causing wide spread destruction in the mining area. At the same time over 50,000 Luxembourgers fled into France. The Germans decreed that the south of the country be evacuated and 50,000 inhabitants were taken to the north. This evacuation, coupled with Hitler's instruction that there be no air raids, does point to a German aim of minimising Luxembourgish civilian casualties.

On Saturday 11th May, the Luxembourgish Parliament heard a protest by the president of the Parliament, Emile Reuter, against the invasion, and a cabinet was established, with the aim of running the organs of state in the absence of the monarch and government. From the day of the invasion until 23rd September 1944 a government in exile was maintained under Prime Minister Pierre Dupong, mostly from London and Canada. On 16th May Parliament met again. Indeed it seemed as if a semblance of political normality might be allowed to flourish as it had done during the occupation of 1914-1918. However the German authorities had other plans.

The German representative von Radowitz informed the Luxembourgish parliament that the Third Reich could not recognise its government, as it had 'sided with the Allies.' A journal was published citing new German laws and regulations to be enforced.

The German delegation rapidly became the focal point of power, and it was from here that the orders to arrest dozens of Luxembourgers were made. The delegation had served as a centre of espionage in the lead up to war and files were kept on likely trouble makers. It was also at the German Delegation that collaborators rallied in the days following the invasion.

On 30th May the Luxembourgish delegation in Paris called up all able-bodied male Luxembourgers resident in France for the formation of a Luxembourg Legion. However the speed of the German invasion of France forced the government in exile to flee to Portugal on 22nd June, before this mobilisation could happen.

In Paris, the Luxembourg-born and Luxembourgish speaking Robert Schuman was still a Deputy in the French parliament. Although he voted to give Marshal Pétain full powers following the German invasion, he quickly distanced himself from the Vichy regime and within the next two months he was arrested by the Gestapo.

In August the government in exile and the royal family arrived in London, where Grand Duke Jean joined the British army, as a private in the Irish Guards.

On 28th June 1940 the Grand Duchy was associated with the German region of Koblenz Trier as a first step towards annexation. Shortly afterwards a high ranking Nazi official arrived in Luxembourg. He was a handsome man, despite his slightly receding hair, which he wore short and greased back. He had a sharp, thin nose, piercing eyes and was impeccably turned out. He was called Gustav Simon, a name that would live on in infamy in the Grand Duchy for decades to come.

Simon was born in 1900 and had joined the Nazi Party in 1925. In 1928 he was appointed *Besirkleiter* or district governor of Trier then, in 1931, he became *Gauleiter* or area commander of the Koblentz-Trier region.

In July 62 year old Damian Kratzenberg was paid German funds to set up the *Volksdeutsch Bewegung*, or ethnic German movement. Kratzenberg was the son of a Luxembourgish mother and German father and was a professor of German at the Athéneum academy. The newly formed VDB enrolled over 84,000 new members, many of German descent, and under the protection of the Reich authorities. The VDB opened offices on the Grand rue at the corner of rue du Fosse from where they co-ordinated recruitment. However, a realistic estimate of genuine volunteer members is probably 5% of this, with the remaining 95% being blackmailed or coerced into joining for professional reasons. This was especially true for civil servants, who were afraid of losing their jobs. In addition Luxembourgers who had enrolled in the *Volksjugend*, the Luxembourgish Nazi youth movement, were presented with the *Golden Youth Badge* by Artur Axmann, the leader of the Hitler Youth.

Over the summer, the authorities moved rapidly to stamp their mark on Luxembourg. On July 25th Gustav Simon was appointed as *Gauleiter*, or governor, of Luxembourg on the orders of Adolf Hitler. Then, on 6th August 1940, the Gestapo and the dreaded *Polizeitruppe*, or German police, took over all policing roles from the local police. The Gestapo based themselves at the Villa Pouly, which soon became a place of dread and terror.

In addition to the secret police and military forces, the Nazi occupiers deployed units of *Wirtschaftstruppen* or 'economic troops' whose job was to scour the country and compile detailed lists of the nation's economic assets, in a Nazi-version of the Doomsday Book. These lists were used to better organise the plunder of Luxembourg's wealth, with the backing of German industrialists.

On 6th August, Simon held an inauguration ceremony in the Place d'Armes, surrounded by 600 police. In his speech Simon set out his plans to purge Luxembourg of what he described as excessive French cultural influence, declaring that Luxembourg was 'too proud of its cultural heritage and its native language to be the parrot of France.' By 'native language' he of course meant German.

German would become the official language under the *Verordnung uber den Gebrauch der deutschen Sprache im Lande Luxemburg,* a decree of 8th August, regarding the German language in Luxembourg. Luxembourish and French were banned, with all publications and education to be exclusively in German. French sounding names were to be changed, including family names. Even the inscriptions on new tombstones had to be in German and it became a crime to say *bonjours* or *merci*. In addition, one of the city's main thoroughfares had its name changed from *avenue de la Liberté* to *Adolf Hitlerstrasse.*

This ban inadvertently helped the Luxembourgish language, Letzebergsch, grow from being a spoken dialect to a written language. Fearful about the survival of the dialect, local speakers wrote it down and agreed spelling and grammar rules. The education minister, Nicolas Welter, had made a start on this task in 1914. However, once writers started trying to produce an underground newspaper they quickly ran into problems and needed to standardise the script. Only once they had started this task could the local resistance publish its secret newspaper, called *D'Un'ion,* in Letzebergsch. The need to actually use the language under pressure forced the pace of phonemic standardisation more than any academic exercise could have done.

On 8th August Luxembourgers were informed that they would henceforth be subject to a new civil legal system rather than military rule. This move ensured a veneer of legality for the Nazi regime but removed from Luxembourgers the scant protection offered to occupied peoples, that the occupying German army had been expected to adhere to.

By early August the Grand Duchess had arrived in London with the government in exile. Her presence was sorely missed as the process of Nazification proceeded apace.

On 13th August civil servants learned that they would need to obey all German orders and to salute the Swastika. In addition, a large number of German civil servants were relocated to Luxembourg. The priority that the occupiers gave to Nazifying the civil service underscores the power of bureaucracy to put into practice genocide and oppression.

On 14th August *Gaulieter* Simon declared the Luxembourgish constitution null and void and any references to the Grand Duchy or State of Luxembourg on any document were banned. All German legislation would be applied to Luxembourg.

The sense of impotent fury and humiliation soon bubbled over and spontaneous crowds gathered to protest. This was met by swift and brutal suppression and hundreds were arrested.

On August 15th Simon abrogated the economic union with Belgium. The German authorities were eager to stamp out economic independence and the *Franc* was replaced with the *Reichmark* a few days later, on 26th August.

During August there were also unsuccessful attempts by the German authorities to incite violence against Jews and every street corner was covered with Nazi propaganda. This did not have the desired effect, Luxembourg having little inclination to anti-Semitism.

On 20th August the dreaded *Sondergericht* was introduced. This was a special Nazi magistrates tribunal with the power to impose death sentences.

On 23rd August all political parties were dissolved and their property seized. Free speech, the right to free assembly and the right to privacy were all outlawed.

A few days later, on 27th August, civil servants learned that they had just one month to sign an oath of allegiance to the Reich. In addition local government was to be radically overhauled and the small town councils replaced with larger units.

On 5th September 1940 the authorities introduced the Nazi racial laws and seized all of Luxembourg's 355 Jewish-owned businesses. *Gauleiter* Gustav Simon ordered the word *Jude* or Jew to be daubed on the windows of all Jewish-owned shops. The Luxembourgish authorities were ordered to purge the civil service of all Jewish civil servants, dentists, doctors and lawyers. Jewish students were expelled from Luxembourgish schools. Non-Jewish Luxembourgish children were to receive two hours a week of 'racial education.'

Nearly 700 Jews managed to flee the country before or just after the invasion. In the autumn of 1940 around a hundred people were given *laissez-passers* by Baron von Hoiningen-Huene, a German citizen who had been resident in the Grand Duchy since 1922, enabling them to escape into France.

Soon after the invasion Luxembourg became an important logistical centre for German troop movements in and out of France and remained so until the fall of France, just as it had done in the 1914-18 conflict.

The German authorities soon began a drive to recruit Luxembourgers into the *Wehrmacht*, the German army. Around 2000 joined voluntarily but most of these were in fact so called Reich Germans, i.e. those with German citizenship. Others were classed as ethnic Germans, that is Luxembourgish citizens of German descent. Before the outbreak of the war 17,000 inhabitants of the Grand Duchy were Reich Germans, out of a population of 290,000.

On 5th September the Grand Duchess gave the first of her talks to the country on the BBC from London. These talks were a source of comfort and hope to Luxembourgers and a source of constant irritation to the Germans. Their response was to employ the services of a William Joyce, better known as Lord Haw Haw because of his plumy voice. Joyce was a British traitor who had been born in New York to Irish-American and English parents. In 1933 Joyce joined the *British Union of Fascists*, becoming Oswald Mosley's deputy. However in 1937 Joyce became a card carrying Nazi and joined the hard-core *National Socialist League*.

By 1939 he was forced to flee to the Reich using a false passport. For much of the war he sent defeatist messages on Radio Hamburg as well as from the radio facilities in Luxembourg.

September was a bad month. Rationing was introduced, following the German system. Then the entire rail network was incorporated into the German *Reichbahn* rail company. On 12th September draconian new laws were announced to deal with anyone found defacing Nazi posters. Then, on 13th September, the German authorities gave the Jews fifteen days to leave the country. If they failed to leave, the authorities threatened to deport them on Yom Kippour, the holiest day in the Jewish calendar. Only intense petitioning by the Jewish consistory, including a letter to Himler, managed to postpone this deadline. Most were only too eager to leave but the problem was finding somewhere to go.

Three days later, on 16th September, laws were passed regulating what Luxembourgers could listen to on radio. Listening to the wrong stations was classed as *reichfeindlich* or anti-German and was severely punished.

On September 29th 1940 the *Volksdeutscher* Movement of Luxembourg held a mass rally and Gustav Simon proclaimed a "new order" for Luxembourg within the Reich. To boost morale Himmler himself paid the local Gestapo a visit.

On 1st October a decree was issued ordering Jews to deposit all their cash into a Luxembourg bank account. Furthermore Jews would only be allowed 250 *Reichsmarks* a month from then on. Coupled with a ban on professional activities by Jews, many were forced to seek official permission to sell their furniture to survive.

On October 4th 1940 the Grand Duchess safely arrived in the United States from England. However in order not to compromise American neutrality it was deemed best for her to move on to Canada, where she set up a government in exile in November 1940, along with Prime Minister Pierre Dupong. The government in exile was represented in London by the Foreign Minister Joseph Bech, who was later to become Prime Minister in a post-war Luxembourg, and by Labour Minister Peter Krier.

During October all Jews lucky enough to have visas for third countries were driven to the border of unoccupied France under Gestapo guard. This amounted to nearly a 1000 people.

During the same period all civil servants were required to complete detailed forms relating to their home life and political opinions. These were then stored and used for information by the Gestapo. At the same time all public places and schools were to be adorned with pictures of Hitler.

On 16th October the historical seat of Luxembourgish democracy, the *Chambres des Députés,* was taken over by a new body known as the propaganda office.

On 20th October the monument called the *Gelle Fra,* commemorating those Luxembourgers killed fighting for France during the Great War, was demolished. It was a symbol the Nazis despised as it negated their claim that Luxembourg was basically a little bit of Germany. The monument stood opposite the site of the present day national library. However, such was the fury that this action provoked that a group of high school students held a spontaneous demonstration, despite the awful personal risks involved. The Gestapo snatched protestors at random, questioned them, beat them up and released them.

On 22ⁿᵈ October a new court was established to try civil servants who did not comply with German orders. The next day the *Gaulieiter* dissolved the Luxembourgish parliament, ending all pretence of co-operation.

On 26ᵗʰ October the politician Albert Werner was 'relieved of his functions' and disappeared.

By the winter of 1940 a credible resistance was being built up. Initially the various resistance groups grew out of different political parties such as the Communists. Others were formed by students or unionists. One problem that all the nascent groups faced however, was a lack of weapons, due to the fact that Luxembourg had been demilitarised for so long. For this reason most resistance was based on circulating information and hiding people, rather than sabotage or assassination. This probably saved Luxembourg from some of the worst atrocities inflicted on other occupied peoples as reprisals for fatal attacks on Germans.

Towards the end of 1940 the process of Nazification was almost completed and three main thrusts were introduced to complete it. This began with a reorganisation of the judiciary on 9ᵗʰ November, followed by new commercial regulations on 12ᵗʰ November, and finally a reorganisation of religious life on 14ᵗʰ December. This drive became known as *Gleichschaltung* or harmonisation.

As the winter drew in, a new organisation was created known as *Winterhilfswerk* or winter aid. Women gathered at street corners with collection tins to raise funds for the needy during the winter. This was a cynical Nazi ploy at controlling charity.

On 2nd January 1941 the artist Joseph Kutter died.

On 5th January 1941 Gustav Simon made an ominous speech in which he vowed to crush and exterminate any resistance to the Reich or the German people. Few doubted he meant every word. Ten days later severe punishments for resistance or sabotage were announced.

In late January 1941 the authorities introduced forced labour, with all manual labourers being enrolled in the *Deutsches Arbeits Front,* a kind of compulsory work force union. This was to facilitate the distribution of workers to areas essential for the Nazi war machine. Those who refused to register were sacked from their existing posts. Under the circumstances generated by the occupation this could result in starvation or severe hardship for the person concerned and their family. All men and women in the 15-21 age group were initially required to register with the *Reichsarbeitsdienst*, the German labour service.

On 31st January a decree obliged all Luxembourgers to Germanise their names. Lists of approved names were circulated.

A week later, on 7th February, all property belonging to exiled Jews was seized under the slogan 'Jewish means are public means.'

On 18th February the typical French beret was banned. This step was also taken in the French province of Alsace, another territory the Nazis intended to Germanise.

Meanwhile, in Paris Robert Schuman was placed under house arrest, in April 1941.

On 16th May 1941 the synagogue on rue de la Congregation was closed down. Ten days later the Chief Rabbi Serebrenik fled the country, fearing for his life. On 3rd June 1941 the synagogue in Esch-sur-Alzette was demolished. During July, the now closed Luxembourg City synagogue was also razed to the ground. Soon afterwards, on 29th of July 1941, a decree was issued, excluding Jews from all walks of life.

In August, work began on preparing a "Jewish retirement home" at the old convent at Cinqfontaines, near Troisvierges, in the north of the country. Cinqfontaines, or Fuenfbrunnen in German, was a dark and foreboding place, perched on a hill above the railway. Over 400 sick or aged Jews were taken there and confined in crowded conditions. The convent was organised as a ghetto, and it was from here that deportations would soon take place by train. The convent was ideal for its purpose. It was isolated, easy to guard and handy for railway sidings. Meanwhile others Jews were forced to work at the Paul Wurth factory, or made to carry out road building.

Despite the enormous risks, resistance bubbled away. On 6th October Nazi officials were outraged to discover that Swastikas had been ripped and left on the ground at a sports ground in Ettelbruck. In the absence of any information about those responsible the authorities took twenty one hostages and then imposed a collective fine of 500,000 *Reichmarks* on the entire town.

Three days later, on 9th October, the press carried news of a death sentence, pronounced on a man from Bettembourg who had attacked a Nazi.

As early as 1940 the German-controlled press had been promoting the slogan "If you don't wish to be my brother I'll break your skull." This was an old German saying, but chillingly it was soon to be put into practice. On 10th October 1941 the German authorities held a census known as the *Personenbestands- und Betriebsaufnahme*, during which the people of Luxembourg were asked several questions. One was about their race or ethnicity, one about their mother tongue and one about which nation they belonged to. The authorities let it be known that the correct answer to all three of these questions would be German. This was a slight change in the pre-war position when Luxembourgers were forbidden from joining the Hitler Youth for example. In the run up to the census the resistance secretly canvassed the population to answer 'Luxembourgish' to all three questions, which they did as an overwhelming majority. This took huge amounts of personal courage as the forms were stamped and needed to be signed and completed by everyone over 16. No-one could be sure that anyone else would refuse to comply with the German wishes. In the countryside over 99% answered Luxembourgish to all questions and in the cities the figure was 96%. The next day the press announced that the census had been scrapped 'for technical reasons.' The spirit of the overwhelming rejection is summed up in the national motto *'mir welle bleive wat mir sin'*, 'we wish to remain whom we are.'

Gauleiter Gustav Simon had been humiliated, having offered Luxembourgers the prize of German citizenship and been snubbed. He wasn't about to forget the slight. Almost immediately there was a crack down on all dissents. Any person deemed an enemy of the regime was liable to be sent to a concentration camp as a political prisoner, a fate which befell nearly 3500 men and 500 women over the course of the war. Of these nearly 700 were executed in concentration camps.

On 13th October there was an outpouring of hatred and rage directed at the Grand Duchess Charlotte and

Luxembourg in the German press.

The authorities vented their rage in several ways. Church property was seized and the Abbey at Clervaux was transformed into a Nazi academy known as the Adolph Hitler School. The chapel of the building was used as a gymnasium, the sacrilege underscoring the hardcore Nazi ideology being taught there. In addition to the desecration of one of the country's holiest places, the Grand Ducal palace was transformed into a Nazi drinking establishment. Such gestures can only be seen as deliberate humiliations.

One of the few means of resistance Luxembourgers had at their disposal was to sabotage production at their factories. Any worker could work slower than usual, and things could be 'lost' or broken without too much personal risk. So successful was this strategy that steel production fell by two thirds. The authorities were impotent and furious. On 13th October collective punishment was announced as a new tool to fight boycotts and other forms of resistance. This move was illegal under international law, a technicality of no consequence to the Nazi occupiers.

On October 14th all Luxembourg Jews were ordered to wear a yellow star on their clothes. On October 15th Alfred Oppenheimer, the leader of the Jewish Council in Metz in France was ordered to assume control of the Luxembourg Jewish Council, known as the *Consistoire*. On the same day a census reported that 750 Jews were left in the country of whom over 80% were 50 years old or more. On 16th October 324 Jews were deported to ghettos in Poland. This was the first and largest transport from the Grand Duchy. Many of those that remained were ordered to continue building work on the convent at Cinqfontaines, in order to increase its capacity. Henceforth Alfred Oppenheimer would be required to sign any orders given to him by the Gestapo. Making the Jews complicit in their own murder was a favourite Nazi humiliation but Oppenheimer was in no position to refuse.

Between October 1941 and September 1943 eight transports with a total of 674 Jews left Luxembourg. In such a small country, with a large German population, escape was very unlikely. However Luxembourgers did try to help, despite great personal risks. One notable figure was Victor Bodson who was in fact a former Minister of Justice. Bodson owned a house in the village of Steinhem close to the river Sure and he rigged up a special device to his car to enable Jews to cross the river where he would then hide them in his home until safe houses had been found for them.

On 16th October the death penalty was proclaimed for all attempting to cross over into France or Belgium illegally. Then, on 30th October, it became a capital offence to join any Nazi movement with the view to spreading enemy views. In addition the punishment for treason would be death. Even lesser actions such as printing or listening to the radio would henceforth be classified as treason and so carry the death penalty. During October, November and December barely a day went by without someone being imprisoned, tortured or even shot.

In November 1941 a list of property to be surrendered by any Jews still remaining was issued. This included bikes, radios, torches, record players, irons and other electrical goods.

The *Gauleiter* and the Gestapo became ever more brutal as 1941 became 1942. On 7th January 1942 the Jews interned at Cinqfontaines were ordered to surrender most of their clothing, a cruel and unnecessary exercise considering the climate and the age of most of the internees. Then, on 18th January, the Gestapo forbade the inmates at Cinqfontaines from going outdoors, from smoking or from reading newspapers.

Morale amongst Luxembourgers rose with the American entry to the war at the end of 1941 and resistance grew.

Resistance however, met with fury. In January 1942 two death sentences were announced in Differdange and Rumelange. In addition eleven men were deported for forced labour. From March 1942 any Luxembourger who was not regarded a 'friend of the Reich' was liable to have their property seized. This of course now included most of the population,

On 1st April 1942 German Civil law officially replaced Luxembourgish law, though this was by now a largely academic exercise.

On 23rd April 1942 twenty seven Jews were deported to Izbica near Lublin. Then, on 12th July, twenty four Jews were deported to Auschwitz and on 26th July twenty seven Jews were deported to Theresienstadt, joined just two days later by a further 159 Jews.

On 31st July 1942 the former Grand Duchess Regent and wife of Grand Duke IV passed away.

In Paris Luxembourg-born former Deputy Robert Schuman managed to escape house arrest in August 1942 and joined the French resistance.

During August 1942 a further 723 Luxembourg Jews were deported, of whom only thirty five survived the war.

On August 30th 1942 Luxembourg was officially

annexed, a move to which the *Gauleiter* had been building up to since the first day of the occupation. The very name Luxembourg was abolished. The official line was that Luxembourgers were in fact ethnic Germans and therefore had a *Heim ins Reich,* a place in the Reich. The local Luxembourgish population were increasingly encouraged to identify as German and propaganda repeatedly alluded to the conflict against the French in the past. The country became known as *Gau Moselland.* The *Gauleiter* henceforth set out to Germanize Luxembourg totally. Luxembourgers in effect became German citizens against their will.

There followed a series of articles in the official press lauding Luxembourgers of yore for their fighting spirit. This set alarm bells ringing for many.

As the Luxembourgers were now German citizens they became subject to German duties, and conscription was introduced for Luxembourgish men in August 1942. Luxembourgers reacted with fury to the annexation and to the introduction of conscription, which was in direct breach of the Hague Convention on the treatment of occupied peoples.

Overnight the resistance circulated tracts calling for a general strike to take place on 31st August 1942. The strike rapidly spread from Ettelbruck and Wiltz in the morning to include the whole country by the afternoon. The *Gauleiter* imposed martial law, rounded up ringleaders and sent them to the concentration camp of Hinzert, just outside the city of Saarbrucken in Germany. Hinzert became Luxembourg's local concentration camp and was used to intern political prisoners from the Trier region of Germany as well as those from the Grand Duchy, Belgium and parts of the Netherlands. The strikers were tried by court martial known as the *Standgericht* and the following day twenty five of them were shot. One other man was taken to the German city of Cologne, where he was beheaded. The death penalty was ordered for all those who refused to return to work. Between 2nd and 8th September 1942 twenty resistance members and dissidents were shot. Young students who had participated were deported to Germany as forced labourers for a year. Such punishment deportations were referred to as *Strafversetzt* in German.

The first call up of Luxembourgish men was for those who had been born between 1920 and 1924. Many ended up on the Russian front as German cannon fodder, and conditions on the Russian front were hellish. Some deserted and joined the Russians. Those that couldn't, and who subsequently fell into Soviet hands, were treated the same as other German POWs by the Soviets and sent to the Tambow POW camp where conditions were appalling. Many of the POWs died of neglect. By the end of the occupation 10,200 men had been conscripted, of whom 2848 were either killed in action or shot as deserters. A further 1500 were severely wounded or maimed.

There were of course some Luxembourgers who served willingly in the German forces. As Luxembourg was now considered part of Germany and not occupied territory there was to be no Luxembourg Legion serving Germany under the Luxembourg flag, and therefore it is hard to separate Luxembourger from German in the various branches of the German war machine. It is known that some Luxembourgers volunteered for the Luftwaffe, the Navy and even the Waffen SS which attracted 110 Luxembourgish recruits.

However many Luxembourgish men fled the

country successfully and were eventually able to reach Britain and join the allied forces or else join the French and Belgian resistance. Secret paths, known only to locals, led through the forests to the borders. Those who could not flee were hidden in cellars, mines, forests or farms and even churches. Roughly two thirds of draft evaders were hidden inside the Grand Duchy. However hiding was a hard decision to make. The penalty for draft evasion and desertion, known in German as *Fahnenflucht*, or for hiding someone, could be death and the deportation, or *Emsiedlung,* of their family. In addition illegal emigration was termed *unbefugte Abwanderung* and attracted the severest penalties.

From 1942 the Nazi actions had the effect of stiffening resistance rather than weakening it, and a dedicated resistance network developed, their main role being to hide Luxembourgish conscripts and shot down allied airmen as well as to sabotage the German war machine.

For those in the resistance, capture meant almost certain death and torture at the hands of the Gestapo. However many did join. One resistance group was known as the *Red Lions*, specialising in hiding conscripts. Another group, the *Patriotic League*, assisted hundreds of Allied airmen to escape capture.

On 9th September 1942 the *Gauleiter* announced the mass deportation of politically undesirable elements from Luxembourg and on 17th September a first batch of Luxembourgish deportees left Hollerich station, in the south of the city, for an unknown destination. The deportees had been carefully selected using lists compiled by Werner Lorenz, the Chief Liaison Officer for Ethnic Germans. As early as the autumn of 1941 Lorenz had been given the task of identifying ethnic Germans in Luxembourg. This came to include all Luxembourgers with no foreign blood. From Lorenz's list, the Nazis then selected those they felt were racially sound but politically hostile for deportation.

On 23rd September fifty families were deported to Germany and Poland. This was followed on 10th October by a further fifty three families. After this date the press simply stopped announcing deportations.

Deportations invariably followed the same ghastly routine. At around 6.00AM the family would be woken by the Gestapo and given three hours to pack. The head of the household would then be forced to hand over the keys to the house, which was then locked and sealed. A yellow poster was attached to the front door. A coach would then pick the family up and drive them to the station. Only hand baggage was allowed and the families, old and young alike, were forced onto trains, bound for Silesia. With the family on its way, the police would return to the home and arrange for the sale of the family's belongings. Often the empty homes were used to house ethnic Germans from the east, as well as German citizens made homeless by allied bombing. Such a policy was designed to lead to an irrevocable intermixing of Germans and Luxembourgers.

In England, the *Luxembourg Society* was formed on 18th November.

Back home, Luxembourgers found themselves being coerced into joining a host of Nazi organisations, though some did so willingly. By the end of 1942 the *Volksdeutsche Bewegung* had 70,000 members, although some brave individuals had returned their membership cards, as a protest against conscription. The SS had 110 Luxembourgish recruits and the SA over 1100. The Hitler

Youth had approximately 9400 members and the National Socialist Women's Movement had nearly 58,000 members. It is however hard to separate the ethnic Germans from the true Luxembourgish members.

In addition to the pro-Nazi groups, 57,650 Luxembourgers had been drafted into the *Deutsches Arbeits Front* or forced labour detachment. These were referred to mockingly as *Beutedeutsche,* or 'booty Germans' by their guards. The Nazi authorities also tried to create, with very limited success, organisations for Nazi Luxembourgers living in Belgium and France.

On 23rd February 1943 all able bodied men between the ages of 16 and 65 were ordered to report for forced labour, along with all unmarried women from 17 to 45.

After the huge German defeat at Stalingrad at the beginning of 1943, Luxembourgers were even more desperate to avoid conscription. It was in this climate of fear and desperation that a riot broke out amongst young Luxembourgish conscripts, assembled at the main station, on March 6th 1943. The Germans, determined not to allow a precedent, quelled the revolt with machine gun fire. Although the authorities were keen to promote the cosy idea of Luxembourgers simply being Germans, it is doubtful that they would have responded to such a protest in this way within Germany. It is also certain that the German authorities realised that Luxembourgish recruits would make bad soldiers. Given the relatively small numbers of troops they could muster in the Grand Duchy and the risk such reluctant soldiers posed to the unity and morale of any unit they were posted to, it seems that conscription had another purpose. It was designed to crush the spirit of Luxembourgers and to hammer home the point that, like it or not, Luxembourg was now part of a Thousand Year Reich from which there would be no escape.

On 25th March the next batch of conscription was introduced for all able-bodied men born in 1925. As with the previous draft, this caused huge amounts of anguish and drove many more young men into hiding, with dire consequences for their families.

Men and women who found themselves drafted into the notorious RAD, or forced labour service, were put at risk of being killed in Allied air raids on German industrial centres, which were increasing in severity. However if the forced labourers did not comply, then their families risked persecution and deportation.

On 6th April 1943 nearly all the remaining ninety Jews at the so-called "Jewish Retirement Home" of Cinqfontaines were deported to Thereisenstadt. Then, on 17th June, Cinqfontaines was finally closed and the last eleven inmates sent to Theresienstadt and thence to Auschwitz. In total 1,945 of the 3500 Jews in Luxembourg in 1940 were killed. The rest had been able to flee before it was too late. Only a handful survived deportation.

On 14th July the government in exile passed a decree spelling out that collaborators would not escape punishment upon liberation, a fact which was broadcast to the country and picked up by those who still had access to radio.

In September 1943 *Gauleiter* Simon Gustav declared Luxembourg *'judenrein'* or cleared of Jews. Some Jews who were married to non Jews managed to escape deportation however. In addition roughly thirty Jews remained hidden by non-Jewish Luxembourgers. A further 500 Luxembourg Jews who had found temporary sanctuary in Belgium and France were later deported and killed.

As the tide turned against Germany on the Russian front, conditions worsened in occupied Luxembourg. Food shortages, lack of fuel and compulsory long hours led to a steel workers strike in November 1943. As one Luxembourger in ten had been deported or conscripted, the German authorities replaced their labour with Spanish fascist volunteers and Polish forced labourers.

Some Luxembourgers were deported to Peenemunde in Germany where they were put to work on Germany's new secret weapon, the V1 rocket. Noticing that one of the guards was a Luxembourgish conscript, the forced labourers managed to give him some plans of the rocket. The guard then smuggled the plans back to Luxembourg when on leave, and handed them to the resistance who in turn gave them to the British.

Another round of conscription was announced on 10th December 1943, this time for all men born in 1926. By now Luxembourgers were at their wits end, faced with the blood sacrifice of a new generation of young men.

During the coming year, the four main resistance groups united to form a single group called *UNION*, in order to better fight the occupation and to hide draft evaders. However the penalties for resistance remained draconian and on 26th February 1944 twenty three men were shot for a variety of anti-German actions.

In March 1944 the government in exile, in agreement with the Free French and the Belgians, set in motion the creation of a Luxembourgish artillery battery under Belgian command. This became known as the Piron Brigade or the Luxembourg Brigade, and was attached to the 1st Belgian Artillery Brigade. Some of the Luxembourgish volunteers in the Piron Brigade were ex-French Foreign Legion and had experience in North Africa. Others were deserters from the *Wehrmacht* who had somehow managed to escape to England. On the eve of the D-Day landings the brigade had three Luxembourgish officers, nine NCOs and sixty eight privates.

On 9th May 1944 residents of Luxembourg City heard the rumble of planes. Minutes later a squadron of American B-17 bombers came into view and proceed to bomb the station's marshalling yards, dropping a total of 133 tons of explosives. Two days later they returned to finish the job, this time dropping 158 tons of explosives. As they left, they saw a 'target of opportunity' in the marshalling yards of Bettembourg station, upon which they released a further 57 tons of explosives. During the raids, some of the local population took shelter in the Casemates, the medieval tunnels in the centre of Luxembourg City. For most however, there simply wasn't time and civilian casualties were appalling. Later, witnesses described some of the victims as being decapitated.

On 14th June the government in exile issued a decree repealing the law of 1881 which capped the armed forces. The decree also made provision for conscription to be introduced upon liberation, negating the treaties upon which modern Luxembourg had been founded.

On 14th July 1944 a final batch of conscription was ordered for all those men born in 1927. The situation for Luxembourgish conscripts was now becoming critical, as the Russian front caved in.

On 19th July the local press announced the execution of nine men for anti-German crimes. The following day a local Nazi was shot dead by a Luxembourger in the town of Junglinster. Three weeks later ten Luxembourgish deserters were executed as revenge.

Meanwhile the government in exile was planning for liberation, and on 27th July the *Civil Affairs Agreement* was reached with the Americans, setting out a detailed liberation plan.

On August 6th 1944 the Luxembourgish Artillery Brigade landed on the Normandy beaches to assist with the liberation of France and Belgium. They were equipped with four 25-pounder guns, with a range of 12km. Each gun was named after a Luxembourgish princess. They were also equipped with a Morris truck for carrying their ammunition. The Luxembourgish Piron Brigade's numbers were augmented during September by another forty six Luxembourgish volunteers, fresh from training in England. A small number of the Piron Brigade then formed an elite scout troop whose job was to infiltrate enemy positions and direct the artillery fire.

Following the D-Day landings there was a new wave of hope and increased resistance, attracting ever harsher German reprisals.

During 1944 the governments in exile of Belgium, Luxembourg and the Netherlands signed an agreement to form an economic union as soon as their countries were freed. This was to have far-reaching effects in the decades following the war. In addition, on 9th August, a Grand Ducal decree was passed in exile, setting out what would happen to the currency upon liberation. It set out an exchange rate for Reichmarks to Belgian francs. Two days later a Grand Ducal decree was issued setting out procedures for the smooth return of deportees and the return of their property. This would be a massive problem, considering the very high percentage of Luxembourgers currently in Germany against their will.

By the end of August the writing was well and truly on the wall for the Nazi authorities and many began packing their bags in readiness to leave. On the night of 31st August and 1st September Gustav Simon fled the country, along with his cabinet of officials and thousands of German civilians. Some Luxembourgish collaborators also left. Every road east out of the country was clogged with jeeps, trucks, cars, taxis and bicycles. This exodus resulted in all civil administration grinding to a halt. The trains and trams stopped running, electricity was cut off and newspapers ceased publication. In the confusion several hundred deportees and forced labourers were able to slip back into the country.

On September 8th German forces completed their pullout from Luxembourg to their new positions behind the Siegfried Line, a long strategic line of defences on the German side of the Moselle and Sure rivers.

By Saturday 9th September liberation was on Luxembourg's doorstep as the first American troops, members of the American First Army led by General Courtney Hodges, crossed the border at the village of Pétange. The troops met little resistance, as nearly all the German troops had retreated. Sunday dawned bright and sunny and by lunch time Luxembourg City was in the hands of the liberators. Crown Prince Jean was present as part of the liberating army, having joined the Irish Guards in 1942. Luxembourgers came out onto the streets to cheer the American 5th Army. This included a number of draft evaders who had been hiding. Unable to contain their joy many Luxembourgers wept. Flags, carefully hidden during the occupation, were hung from every window and jeeps and tanks were strewn with flowers as the troops gave out gum and sweets, relishing the attention.

However, there were other emotions too. Now that the country was in Allied hands there could be no reuniting of families, and deported relatives would remain trapped behind German lines until the end of the war, whenever that might be. This was an emotional torture affecting a huge proportion of the tiny nation. 3000 Luxembourgers still languished in concentration camps, 7000 were in the German army, 1500 were performing forced labour and a further 4000 had been deported to eastern Germany and Silesia.

By September 12th the entire country had been liberated and American forces reached the border with Germany.

In the absence of a government, the country was run by the *US Civil Affairs Committee*, and order maintained by a collection of Allied troops and Luxembourgish resistance fighters. Lt Col Edgar Jett was given the job of restoring public services and maintaining public order. The leadership of the US 18th Army Group took over premises opposite the main railway station, from where they co-ordinated troop movements.

Luxembourg became something of a rest and recreation base for American soldiers recuperating from the conflict. Meanwhile, Radio Luxembourg's facilities were used to transmit coded messages to agents in Germany. However the Siegfried Line was far from quiet and the battle not yet won. All along the front line Germans artillery repeatedly shelled Luxembourgish towns, notably Remich and Grevenmacher. In addition to the shelling, German raiding parties made forays into border towns such as Echternach and caused indiscriminate damage. For this reason the area was evacuated and became known as the 'Ghost Front'. Even Luxembourg City itself was a mere 45-minute drive to the front. In addition, much of the north of the country was evacuated, with the evacuees finding accommodation in the capital city, the south or even in Belgium.

Within days of the liberation all Nazi laws were formally repealed.

On 23rd September four senior members of the government in exile arrived back home, including the former Prime Minister Pierre Dupong and foreign minister Joseph Bech.

On 14th October the currency was formally changed to the Belgian Franc and citizens queued to change their Reichmarks.

On 30th November compulsory military service for Luxembourgers was introduced by Grand Ducal decree. Luxembourgers would serve in Allied armies as required.

During September and October the German forces had been regrouping behind the Siegfried Line which separated Germany from the Allied front, and secret orders were issued that all Luxembourgers and Belgians be removed from locations near the front-line inside Germany. Despite their new German citizenship the authorities obviously mistrusted the drafted Luxembourgish conscripts and forced labourers in their midst. By mid-December Operation *Abwehr*, also known as X-Day or Autumn Fog, was ready and plans drawn up for night-time river crossings at Roth, Bollendorf,

Wallendorf and Echternach.

At around five o'clock on the morning of Saturday December 16th 1944 the German Sixth Panzer Division began a massive and sustained artillery bombardment along the western front. Half an hour later, special assault troops began their advance, using temporary bridges. Continued bombardment was used to soften up the American positions, along with blinding floodlights. The strategy behind the German offensive was summed up in two words; surprise and speed. The Wehrmacht then proceeded with a devastating attack, forcing their way into the Ardennes. German forces poured back into the north of the Grand Duchy, to the dismay of the newly liberated population.

Using massed Panzer divisions, elite Waffen SS shock troops, and the notorious *Organization Todt*, the Germans, under Field Marshal von Rundstedt opened up a sixty mile front. In order to penetrate American lines, the Germans also deployed commandos dressed as G.I.s, whose mission was to sabotage the American positions from within. The Americans later executed these commandos, deeming their behaviour to be against international conventions.

The German forces focused their initial attack on a line stretching from Hosingen to Diekirsch, then pushed down onto Ettelbruck and Mersch. Vianden fell relatively easily, and by the afternoon of the 16th the town was once again in German hands. Ettelbruck fell less easily, with the Germans sustaining heavy casualties from American mortar fire. This hindered the German advance over their temporary bridges. Echternach also proved tough for the Germans to reoccupy due to the craggy terrain and fierce resistance. Nevertheless the Germans soon carved out a bridgehead around Dickweiler. One American success though, was to disrupt the German crossing at Waldbillig and Wallendorf.

The main targets for the advancing Germans were pockets of American artillery, including a concentration of troops at Medernach and Altrier. The American artillery were spoiling the German plans and this resistance had to be smashed before the Germans would be free to proceed into Belgium.

Over the next two days the Americans were forced to retreat from about a third of the Grand Duchy and poor weather meant they could not make use of air support. For many of the Luxembourgish inhabitants in the north who had not fled, the American retreat meant deportation and even execution at the hands of the Waffen SS units who ruthlessly flushed out resistance. It was these troops who later carried out the notorious massacre of American prisoners at Malmédy in Belgium days later. The northern third of Luxembourg had become a savage battle arena.

By 19th December the American 28th Division were forced to flee Wiltz in the north, after an heroic two-day stand which left much of the historic town in ruins. However, this resistance delayed the German advance on the Belgian town of Bastogne, which was critical for the battle.

Despite some success at Wiltz, the Americans suffered a serious defeat at Harlange, in the north west of the Grand Duchy, on 19th December. The Germans managed to capture hundreds of American troops, and forty tanks, which the Germans then put to use. Christnach and the Mullerthal valley also fell that day.

Ettelbruck fell to the Germans on 21st December. However the attack on Luxembourg was not going as planned, due to stiff American resistance. Moreover morale was low, following the death of General Major Mohring, who had been shot near Beaufort. Planned Waffen-SS reinforcements were not materialising and many bridges remained unusable.

As the Germans continued to mop up resistance in Luxembourg, the Americans diverted their Third Army from a planned attack on the Saar region of Germany, under the command of the formidable General Patton. The American counter-offensive began on 21st December. It was ferocious, and had the advantage of drawing on fresh troops. Patton hit back hard, concentrating the American counter-offensive on and around Wiltz. On 22nd December the Mullerthal fell to the Americans.

On 23rd December a major and savage battle erupted around the towns of Martelange and Arsdorf. The following day what was left of Martelange fell to the Americans. It is hard to imagine the sheer terror felt by any inhabitants left in the north of the country, as the battle ebbed and flowed around them. Families cowered in cellars for days on end, often unsure if their homes were occupied by the Americans, the Waffen SS or neither.

On 24th December the Americans liberated Ettelbruck, one of the largest towns in the north. To this day many walls in the town are peppered with bullet holes.

Meanwhile, the government launched a national fund from the relative safety of the capital, named after the Grand Duchess. This set out to supplement the incomes of those families torn apart by the war and was unveiled on Christmas Day.

After Christmas an improvement in the weather gave the Third Army the advantage, allowing them, once again, to rely on air support.

By 26th January German forces had withdrawn from Echternach, leaving the ancient town in ruins and the historic abbey seriously damaged.

Martelange and the surrounding area was the scene of renewed fighting on 27th December. On New Year's Eve the Germans were forced out of Boevange by devastating American artillery fire. Then, on New Year's Day, the village of Doncols came under American bombardment in an effort to harass and isolate the Germans in nearby Wiltz. A German pocket remained cut off near Martelange and renewed attempts were made to free them.

On 2nd January a front line developed from Grumelscheid to Lutrebois. The Germans pulled back slightly in order to regroup for a possible attack on the American fortress at Bastogne. To this end they set up bases at Grumelscheid station and at Noertrange.

On 4th January German forces regrouped at Kautenbach but this was disrupted when the Americans launched a surprise attack on the villages of Goesdorf and Dahl. At Dahl the Germans counter-attacked, throwing every available piece of artillery at the Americans but this failed when they ran out of ammunition.

On 9th January the Americans broke the German lines at Bevigne, followed by a breakthrough at Doncols two days later.

By 12th January the German High Command decided to withdraw its forces back behind the Siegfried Line. However, in order to do this successfully they needed to withdraw slowly and therefore they had to fight back fiercely. The terrain stretched their resourcefulness to the limit and in the end the German forces were required to evacuate much of their equipment, including field kitchens, by hand through the forests.

On 12th January fierce fighting took place near the Nassau dynasty's ancestral seat of Vianden, and at Hoscheid.

On 13th January the Germans made an organised retreat to the forests around Wiltz and Clerf. Both places were seen as vital in order to organise an orderly escape.

Diekirch came under American attack on 18th January after a night crossing of the river Sure by American forces. On 21st January the town was secure.

On 20th January the village of Brandenbourg fell, followed by Clerf on 25th January. Some of the worst fighting was centred on the village of Pintsch, which was quickly reduced to ruins. The following day, on 26th January, the devastated town of Hoscheid briefly fell back into German hands. On January 26th the Americans had reached the German border but several German bridgeheads remained in Luxembourgish territory, clustered around Vianden and Gemund, as well as at Hosingen, Putscheid and Weiler. It was vital for the Germans to hold these as long as possible in order to allow their embattled forces to escape behind the Siegfried Line. The last gasp of German resistance on Luxembourgish soil took place at Dasburg and Gemund, which finally fell on 31st January.

The Beast was gone.

The cost of the Battle of the Bulge was huge, with nearly 75,000 American casualties, many of whom died from exposure or their wounds. In response, a massive new cemetery was opened on 29th December at Hamm, five km from the capital. In addition, 5599 German dead were buried at the village of Sandweiler by the US Army Burial Service.

Luxembourg's war was over. However, nearly one home in five had been destroyed leaving 60,000 homeless Luxembourgers. In addition over 160 bridges and tunnels had been wrecked by one or other side. One tragedy was the partial destruction of chateau of Clervaux, which was hit by a German incendiary bomb.

By early spring the American authorities began allowing refugees back into the Ardennes area where they found their homes devastated and many of their neighbours dead, some of them murdered by the Waffen SS.

In March 1945 the government set about creating a more organised Luxembourgish army and established the *Compagnie de la Garde Grand Ducale* at the Saint Esprit barracks in the capital.

On 14th April Grand Duchess Charlotte returned home, along with her government in exile. This was a moment of intense joy and a reassurance that for Luxembourg the war was over. Meanwhile rule by decree was continued until elections could be held.

On April 30th Prince Felix was shown around the concentration camp at Dachau, near Munich, where he met Luxembourgish survivors, mostly resistance fighters and dissidents.

In addition to the return of the royal family, thousands of deportees, and some concentration camp survivors, began to drift back from Germany. Luxembourgers were confronted with the true horror of what had befallen them. Many were deeply traumatised and found it hard to adjust.

On June 26th Luxembourg signed the United Nations Charter. This was ratified on August 10th.

In July 1945 a first and second infantry battalion was created, based in Walferdange and Duddeldange.

By the winter, many of the Luxembourgish POWs began to return from the Soviet Union. Out of 1000 captured alive by the Russians only 840 returned. Their captivity had been horrific, with pitiful food, brutality and biting cold. In addition, they had felt the shame and irony of being labelled as Nazi soldiers when they had been drafted against their will.

As well as the POWs, some of the fifteen hundred Jews who had fled to safety during the early stages of the occupation, began to return, reopening what was left of their businesses. Luxembourg was unusual for an occupied country, in that its post-war Jewish population was similar in size and composition to its pre-war one.

By the end of the war a total of 5259 Luxembourgish citizens had lost their lives. Yet despite the huge losses in both human lives and architectural heritage, Luxembourgers were determined to get their country back on its feet as soon as possible. By the end of 1945 some rebuilding was underway on damaged monuments, including the historical fin de siècle Abbey of Ss Maurice and St Maur at Clervaux. In addition the *Monument du Souvenir*, known in Luxembourgish as the *Gelle Fra*, was rebuilt. This was a memorial to the dead of the First World War, which the Germans had demolished in 1940.

During November the Luxembourgish army was deployed in the French zones of occupation in western Germany, notably around the cities of Saarburg and

Bitburg. This deployment illustrated Luxembourg's wider commitment to the security of Europe.

Just what was it that had driven Germany to invade its tiny, peaceful neighbour for the second time? Germany's reasons for invading Luxembourg initially appeared to be the same as their reasons in 1914. France's border was heavily protected by the Maginot Line, and the only undefended route into France was therefore through Belgium and Luxembourg. Yet once France had been subdued it would have been possible for German troops to withdraw with minimum risk. Unlike the Netherlands or Belgium, Luxembourg had no coast to guard. Might it not have been in Germany's interests to have a small, neutral, landlocked state on her doorstep? After all, Germany did not have any interest in invading Switzerland, or Sweden. A neutral Luxembourg would have been surrounded by German-controlled territory on all sides and entirely dependent on the good will of the Reich. For this reason alone Germany could have been reassured that the territory would not be used as a haven for escapees or for spying. Luxembourg would have been forced to trade with Germany for its own survival and therefore its valuable natural resources and steel production would have been assured for Germany. Moreover, it could have served as a useful channel of communication and financial dealing. Hitler's early orders indicated that he did not initially intend to invade Luxembourg and in the years prior to the invasion Josef Goebbels stated "If anyone asks today how we imagine the new Europe, we must say we do not know." However once a war with the west became inevitable, Nazi ideology changed. By the time Gustav Simon had been installed as *Gauleiter* the path was clear and Simon stated categorically:

> *On the day when the first grave for a German hero-soldier was dug, we made the following decision: This land was won and will be kept by German blood and therefore will remain German for all eternity.*

It seems therefore that the invasion of 1940 was a deliberate act of conquest and that the intention had been to annex Luxembourg even before the invasion began, for ideological reasons. The cumulative nature of the Nazification process indicates a level of pre-planning.

This conclusion is not without some question marks however. If Nazi ideologues believed Luxembourg and its people were indeed ethnic Germans, why did they treat them with such contempt? Was the plan to erase all traces of a separate Luxembourgish identity as quickly and brutally as possible? Did the Nazis truly expect Luxembourgers to embrace the Reich? In other conquered lands the Nazis used imagery that built upon the history of the subjected nation to reinforce its place in the Aryan orbit. Thus in Norway and Denmark SS recruiting posters juxtaposed SS Scandinavian troops with Vikings. A similar approach was used in the Netherlands and Belgium. In France anti-British sentiment was stirred up, to show the French that they were fighting the wrong side. In Luxembourg it is true that the Luxembourgers were made citizens of the Reich. Yet in the run up to the invasion the local Nazi cells were only open to Reich Germans and not Luxembourgers. They were not it seems entirely trusted. And if this was so, why were they given German citizenship, unlike the other 'Ayran' nations for example the Danes?

After the defeat of the Reich, former *Gauleiter* Gustav Simon went into hiding in Germany. He was later captured in Paderborn, having assumed a false identity, but although Luxembourg asked for his extradition to face a Luxembourgish court he was found hanged in his cell. Rumours circulated that it was not suicide. The infamous Lord Haw Haw was also captured and hanged by the British. He became the last Briton to ever be hanged under the Treason Act.

Elections were held on 21st November 1945, returning the Christian Socialists and their coalition partners to power under Prime Minister Pierre Dupong. The Christian Socialists represented a moderate platform based on Catholic social doctrine. They were to remain in power in one form or another for the next fifty years, reflecting the Catholic and centrist tendencies of the Luxembourgers.

One of the country's first post-liberation acts was to put 1200 collaborators on trial. Top of the list was leader of the *VBD*, Damian Katzenberg. Katzenberg, along with eleven others, were convicted of treason and sentenced to death. Of these, eight death sentences were actually carried out and the others commuted to life in prison. This was the last time Luxembourg would ever use the death penalty. Other collaborators were simply dismissed from government posts. On the streets some women were labelled as collaborators for befriending German soldiers and ostracised. In a country as small as Luxembourg news of such outcasts spread fast and memories were long.

Shortly before Christmas 1945 General Patton, the American war hero, was seriously wounded in a jeep accident in Germany. He struggled with death for nine days but eventually succumbed to his injuries, reputedly muttering the words "a hell of a way for a soldier to die." On Christmas Eve he was laid to rest at the huge cemetery near Hamm. To this day General Patton is fondly remember by Luxembourgers for the liberation of their homeland, and a major road is named in his honour.

Chapter Eight: From the forties to the sixties

The mid 1940s were a time of flux and new beginnings. One major change concerned the approach to the country's local language. On 5th June 1946 a decree made official the *Lezebuurjer Ortografi* or spelling rules. This was an attempt at standardising the anarchic spelling of the Luxembourgish language. This followed on from the work carried out by Jean Feltes, a phonetician. Feltes had been commissioned to do this task by education minister Nicolas Margue. However, the new spelling system didn't really take off. Even a non Letzebuergesch speaker can notice immediately that the name of the language is now spelt *Letzebuergesch* and not *Lezebuurjersch,* such were the difficulties in creating spelling rules for the language.

Another shift in attitude was the approach to defence and neutrality. On July 15th 1946 the size of the army was fixed at 2159, as part of a major overhaul. A military band was organised and the new army consisted of two infantry divisions and a royal guard. On the same day British wartime leader, Sir Winston Churchill, was given the freedom of Luxembourg in recognition of his decisive role in beating Nazi Germany and setting Luxembourg free.

Meanwhile American army grave diggers and landscape gardeners were busy working on the huge cemetery at Hamm. During 1946 over 200,000 visitors came to pay their respects, a mixture of relatives, soldiers and Luxembourgers.

In August 1946 former Socialist resistance leader Albert Winghert was arrested for conspiring to overthrow the Christian Socialist government. Winghert, a former school teacher, was frustrated at the lack of a purge of Nazi collaborators from the civil service. The whole event was slightly farcical and melodramatic. Luxembourg, it seemed, just wasn't a revolutionary kind of country.

That month Luxembourg celebrated the 500th anniversary of the death of Jan the Blind, issuing stamps to commemorate the event. National events and celebrations became an important way of exorcising the wounds and humiliation left by occupation.

Another way in which Luxembourg could gain some justice was by going on the diplomatic offensive and, in November 1946, the Grand Duchy demanded 235 square miles of German territory as compensation. This was not granted by the Allies, although there was some justification in the claim. Huge swathes of Luxembourg had been hived off during earlier treaties including some territory to Prussia. It was this reduction in strategic depth that made tiny Luxembourg so utterly defenceless. Moreover other Allied states were given some territory in compensation. It seemed that Luxembourg didn't have the clout to press the demand any further.

Huge amounts of hard work continued to be put into rebuilding the nation's shattered infrastructure, and farming was increasingly mechanised. One of the most vital sectors of the economy was of course steel making, and for a brief period Luxembourg was able to climb back from sixth place into seventh in the league of world steel producers.

The Jewish community resumed a more structured religious life with the appointment of rabbi Katzenstein in 1946. Life was slowly returning to normal, but many Luxembourgish Jews keenly felt the trauma of the

Holocaust. A small number made their way to Israel in later years.

In September 1946 Radio Luxembourg resumed its popular English language broadcasts, although this time without the help of Lord Haw Haw.

In the same year a small airport began functioning at Findel, on the site of the pre-war airfield and former American airforce base.

In 1947 a census took place, recording a solid Catholic majority of 98.3%. The small non-Catholic minority consisted mainly of Lutherans and Calvinists, with a tiny smattering of Jews.

On 29th October 1947 Luxembourg, Belgium and the Netherlands ratified a customs unions between their countries, as a precursor to the later Benelux Union. The union formally came into force on 1st January 1948 and would evolve into the formal Benelux agreement in 1958.

In November Luxembourg-born Robert Schuman became Prime Minister of France, after having served in the French resistance during the war. The following year Schuman became the Foreign Minister, and it is during this time that he prepared the *Schuman Plan* for the pooling of Europe's coal and steel resources. The plan was unveiled two years later in March 1950.

Like many Western European countries Luxembourg also benefited from joining the American Marshall Plan, which gave aid to the newly liberated countries, in order to promote stability in Europe. This aid was to prove critical in restoring the country to prosperity.

The aid was vital to rebuild the country's infrastructure. One area that required urgent attention was the transport system. Roads had been torn apart by tanks and shelling, railways bombed from the air and many bridges blown up. As part of the overall investment programme, the tiny airport at Findel was given a terminal in 1948. The following year a control tower was added. Nevertheless, for most travellers the train remained the only viable form of long-distance transport. By the late 1940s there was a growing demand for improved communication with other European capitals and in 1948 the *Luxembourg Airlines Company* was formed, based at Findel.

Meanwhile, only a few kilometres from Findel, at Hamm, work began on the grisly task of exhuming more than 5000 American war dead whose families had requested their return to the United States. For much of 1948 the cemetery was closed off and covered with sheets of tarpaulin, in order to shield the grave diggers from public view. Once exhumed, the lead-coated coffins were shipped to the Belgian port of Antwerp for the final journey home. In addition to the exhumations at Hamm, many American war dead were exhumed from graves in France and brought to the better cemetery in Luxembourg. Once the work was completed 5076 American soldiers lay buried in the cemetery, with General Patton's grave moved to the head of his men. A monument by the American architects Voorhees, Walker, Foley and Smith was added in later years to complete the cemetery.

On March 13th Luxembourg, the Netherlands and Belgium agreed to strive for full economic union. This was to become a reality within a decade.

On March 17th 1948 Luxembourg, along with Great Britain, France, Belgium and the Netherlands, signed the Treaty of Brussels, a fifty year treaty of mutual military assistance.

The following year, on April 4th 1949, Luxembourg buried its neutrality for good and joined NATO, realising that neutrality would never guarantee its security. Within the space of only a few years, Luxembourg had tied herself inextricably into a web of alliances and pacts.

In 1950 a new dictionary of the Luxembourgish language was commissioned. This time the spelling used was more similar to German and was the result of a great deal of research into the phonetics and orthography of the language. As a result, it was more successful than the Feltes plan in 1945.

In October 1950 a joint Belgian Luxembourg military force was assembled at Beverloo for action in the Korean war and underwent intensive training. Luxembourg was determined to at least show a symbolic force, perhaps in an attempt to rub away some of the feeling of impotence inflicted during the occupation. In December 1950 the force set sail from Antwerp and became known as the *Belgian United Nations Command*. The force arrived in Korea on 31st January 1951 and was then attached to a US division. Forty three Luxembourgers were present in the joint brigade, which stayed until September 1951 when it was replaced by a second contingent from Luxembourg, formed of forty six volunteers. The brigade was involved in fierce fighting at the battles of Haktang and Chatkol on the Imjin river. Two Luxembourgers were killed in action and a further seventeen wounded.

In April 1951 Luxembourg joined the *European Coal and Steel Community*, the ECSC. This was the culmination of years of work by Luxembourg-born Robert Schuman, the architect of the pact. The agreement established joint authority over the iron, steel and coal industries of France,

Belgium, Germany, the Netherlands and Luxembourg. This was vital to Luxembourg as the steel industry accounted for 75% of the country's industrial output and up to 25% of its GNP.

In 1951 a second group of American Mennonites settled in the Grand Duchy, following in the steps of the first group which had arrived over a hundred years earlier in 1844. This time however, the community settled in the industrial centres of Esch and Dudeldange, rather than the historic town of Echternach.

The 1950s saw an increasing diversification in the Luxembourgish economy, with a distinct shift from heavy industry, such as steel production, to a more service and financial based economy.

The rail network was cut back drastically in the early post-war years, reducing the tracks from over 550km to just under 275 km. This reflected the increasing use of road transport as well as a move away from heavy industry. This of course resulted in some communities becoming isolated and less accessible, in addition to reducing feeder services to the main network.

The early 50s also saw the beginning of Luxembourgish TV broadcasting in French, in black and white, though few families had the luxury of a TV set just yet.

In 1951 Luxembourgish American photographer, Edward J Steichen, conceived of a huge photographic project known as the *Family of Man*. He invited contributions from all over the world, both from established photographers and members of the public. From the two million photographs he selected first 10,000 and then 503 pictures from over 270 contributors. The photographs included birth, children, peace, war, and many other themes of humanity. During the next two decades the exhibition drew nine million visitors. Despite this, the Luxembourgish government decided not to host the exhibition as part of its world tour. It took ten years for Steichen to come to terms with the rebuff.

In 1952 Echternach Abbey was finally reconsecrated after being heavily damaged in the war. The town remained an important spiritual centre.

In May 1952 Luxembourg, along with Germany, France, Italy, the Netherlands and Belgium formed the *European Defence Community*, which was backed up by NATO guarantees.

In the same year Luxembourg became the venue for negotiations between the fledgling state of Israel and the Federal Republic of Germany, over the issue of reparations for the material damage suffered by the Jewish people at the hands of the Nazis. These talks reached their conclusion on the 11th September when $865, 000,000 was offered to Israel and was accepted. The meetings were held in virtual secrecy due to the vehement opposition to the deal by right-wing Israelis. The press were kept outside during the thirteen minute signing ceremony, which took place in stony silence. Journalists were ferried to the City Hall venue without being told where it was and afterwards the two leaders of Israel and Germany were kept hidden away in a room.

There were also negotiations between the governments of Luxembourg and the Federal Republic of Germany over arrangements for the burial of more than 10,000 German dead on Luxembourgish soil. In 1952 agreement was reached regarding the mass graves at the village of Sandweiler, and work began on beautifying the site and arranging a fitting military cemetery. However it was not feasible to exhume and rebury the nearly 5000 soldiers who lay in a mass grave so this was given an appropriate memorial and left as it was.

On 10th August the first session of the high authority of the *European Coal and Steel Community* took place, in the Grand Duchy. Another development in this very international year was opening of the *European Court of Justice* in Luxembourg, one of several European institutions to be located in the Grand Duchy.

On 9th April 1953 the heir to the throne, Hereditary Grand Duke Jean, married Princess Josephine-Charlotte of Belgium. In turn Josephine Charlotte became the Hereditary Grand Duchess. This marriage of course further strengthened the bond between Belgium and Luxembourg.

In 1953 Luxembourg became the seat of the *European Defence Council*.

On 22nd December 1953 Joseph Bech was elected as Prime Minister, following the death of former wartime leader Pierre Dupong.

It was around this time that future Prime Minster Pierre Werner was beginning his rise to power, becoming commissioner for bank control and then Minister of Finance in 1953. Pierre Werner, who was born in Lille to Luxembourgish parents, was passionate about the concept of uniting Europe through a single currency, a vision that was to stay with him all his life. Werner speculated that such a currency would be known as the *euror*. During the occupation Werner had worked for the *Banque General du Luxembourg* but was dismissed by the Nazis.

In 1953 an amnesty was granted for collaborators

and this allowed many to return to posts in the civil service. This move was necessary for the smooth running of the country but for many Luxembourgers it stuck in the throat.

On 30th May 1954 the CSV party scraped just enough seats together to form a coalition government, allowing Joseph Bech to remain in office.

In the same year American actress of Luxembourgish decent Loretta Young, formally Gretchen Michaela Young, won an Emmy. Also in 1954 Radio Luxembourg's name was changed to CLT, *Compagnie luxembourgeoise de telediffusion*.

Luxembourg's armed forces were regrouped in 1954, and offered as a contribution to NATO. These forces included infantry battalions, artillery units, a medical Corp and a transport corps, along with a communication unit and a reconnaissance unit. At this stage, Luxembourg's armed forces totalled nearly 5000 men and the headquarters of the force were located in the village of Walferdange. Training centres were located in Diekirch and in Walferdange, with technical support units located in Capellen and Waldhof. Plans were put in place to boost the total number of troops to over 10,000 in the event of war.

In the same year the *General Patton Bridge* was opened in the devastated town of Ettelbruck. The town fondly remember the ornery General and his role in freeing their town from the Germans.

In 1955 the Remich to Luxembourg City rail link was closed down. This was a blow to the town as well as to the town of Mondorf, which was also served by the line, although the route had been loss-making for a number of years.

In 1955 Luxembourg finally withdrew her troops from the zone of occupation in Bittburg, as well as from Korea, and the joint Belgian-Luxembourgish force for Korea was dissolved in August 1955. A monument to the brigade was erected by the Korean government at Dong-Du-Chon.

During the same year, the German military cemetery at Sandweiler was completed and an opening ceremony held, attended by over 2000 relatives of the dead soldiers, along with government officials.

In 1956 cyclist Charly Gaul became internationally famous by winning the *Giro d'Italia* bike race. That year Luxembourg, always at the forefront of European integration, joined in the first ever *Eurovision Song Contest*, predictably singing in French rather than Letzebuergesch.

In 1956 a small museum was opened in the city of Esch-sur-Alzette, focusing on Luxembourg's wartime resistance movement.

The same year saw the opening of the *Anglican Church of Luxembourg*, under the *Diocese of Europe*.

One of the most significant events in 1956 however, was the changing of the constitution, allowing the government to temporarily transfer sovereign powers to supranational organisations. This was a vital first step towards political union in the European Community.

In November 1956 a crowd of protestors stormed the Soviet embassy, furious at that country's invasion of Hungary. The embassy was hosting a reception at the time the protestors broke in, and shocked delegates watched in horror as furniture was thrown from the windows and then set alight in the grounds.

On March 25th 1957 Luxembourg became one of the six founding members to sign up to the European Economic Community, with the Community coming into being on 1st January 1958. From its conception the Community's goal was ever-closer political and economic integration, a vision to which Luxembourg whole-heartedly subscribed.

On 3rd February 1958 the Benelux Treaty of Luxembourg, Belgium and the Netherlands was signed at the Hague. This represented a terrific achievement and was a forerunner for European political and monetary union. The treaty, which had been in planning even before the end of the war, allowed for the free movement of services, goods and people between the three states. However it was only Belgium and Luxembourg who had a joint currency, with the Netherlands retaining the Guilder. The treaty came into effect in 1960, and was a fast track to wider European integration, four decades before the advent of the single European currency.

In 1958 Robert Schuman was elected president of the European Assembly in Strasbourg where he campaigned for the cause of European unity.

In March 1958 Pierre Frieden replaced Joseph Bech as Prime Minister. Meanwhile the CSV remained in power and Joseph Bech later rejoined the cabinet as foreign secretary.

In the same year Luxembourger Charly Gaul won the prestigious *Tour de France* bike race. This was a rare sporting victory for the European Community's smallest state and the cause of much jubilation and pride.

The iron mines at the industrial southern town of Rumelange closed in 1958. This marked the end of an era, and the beginning of the decline in the industrial sector, upon which Luxembourg had built its economic strength.

In the same year the *Eglise Protestante Néerlandaise*, the Dutch Protestant Church, was opened to cater for the small but growing Dutch community in Luxembourg. Many of the Dutch had arrived in the country shortly before the independence of Belgium in 1830.

On 26th February 1959 Pierre Werner of the CSV was elected Prime Minister. Outgoing Prime Minister Pierre Frieden died the same year. Werner remained in power for the next fifteen years, overseeing the transformation of Luxembourg from an industrial economy to a financial one.

Chapter Nine: The 1960s and 1970s

In March 1960 the audience at London's Festival Hall listened as Camillo Felgen sang in Letzebuergesch for the first time, at the *Eurovision Song Contest*. His song, *So Laang We's Du Do Bast,* came last. Nevertheless it demonstrated a growing willingness to move away from French as the sole language of culture, and a growing Luxembourgish assertiveness.

On 4th July 1960 the American cemetery at Hamm was the site of a memorial service led by American president Eisenhower and Grand Duchess Charlotte.

During the same year, remains of a Merovingian cemetery were unearthed beneath the church at Diekirch. This discovery provided useful evidence about the Frankish period of Luxembourg's history.

The 12th century church at Saeul to the northwest of the capital was comprehensively restored in Romanesque style in 1960.

On 1st November 1960 the Benelux Economic Union, in planning since the early 1930s, came into effect.

In 1961 it was decided to move the national celebrations from 23rd January, which was the birthday of Grand Duchess Charlotte, to a more climatically pleasant 23rd June. Prior to this, the national holiday always coincided with the birthday of the ruling monarch.

In 1961 Edward Steichen held an exhibition of photography called *Steichen The Photographer*, recapping on the events of his life.

On 18th March all eyes were on Luxembourg, when her Eurovision entry, *Nous Les Amoureux,* won for the first time in the country's history. Luxembourg would win a total of five times before dropping out of the contests in 1994. For Luxembourg, Eurovision was one of the few ways of achieving international prestige and winning an international competition, the country being too small to support a world class football team or to draw on a pool of top athletes.

In 1962 Luxembourg hosted the *Cyclo-Cross* world championships.

In the same year the Grand Duchy hosted the seventh *Eurovision Song Contest* on 18th March. This was held at the *RTL Auditorium* at the Villa Louvigny, and was presented by Mireille Delanoy. Camillo Felgen, who had sung in Letzebuergisch two years earlier in London, sang once again for Luxembourg but this time he did it in French. He came third.

In 1962 the *Luxembourg Airlines Company* was reorganised to form *Luxair,* soon to become one of the country's most recognised companies. The airline launched its first regular route from Findel to Paris using a Fokker Friendship F27. Direct services to London were also introduced.

In 1963 the jet age came to Luxembourg when the first jet landed at Findel airport causing much excitement. The feeling that a modern age was dawning was underscored by the construction of a huge dam on the river Our in the same year, along with a massive reservoir on Mont St Nicolas, above the town of Vianden.

In 1963 the *American Luxembourg Society* was

founded in Chicago, which had become one of the biggest centres of Luxembourg-American life. The ties between the two countries were particularly close in the post-war decades.

Robert Schuman died on 4th September 1963, near Metz, receiving tributes from all over the world. He had worked tirelessly to bring the EEC into being and his input would be sorely missed.

In 1963 Grand Duchess Charlotte arrived in Washington on a tour, where she met American-Luxembourgish photographer Edward J Steichen. This marked a change in attitude towards the artist by his compatriots. In 1964 he donated his exhibition *The Family of Man* to the Grand Duchy which was later housed at the Chateau of Clervaux. During his life Edward Steichen married four times, served in two world wars, and served as director of photography at the Museum of Modern Art in New York.

On 12th November 1964 Grand Duchess Charlotte abdicated in favour of her son, Hereditary Grand Duke Jean, who immediately assumed the title of Grand Duke. Whilst Charlotte was adored by her subjects it was believed by some that it would benefit the monarchy for the Grand Duke to take the throne when still young enough to make an impact.

Luxembourg got another turn in the limelight in March 1965, when it won the *Eurovision Song Contest* for the second time. The song, *Poupée de Cire, Poupée de Son*, was written by Serge Gainsbourg and sung by France Gall in French. Coincidentally France Gall was French and so was Serge Gainsbourg. This didn't bother anyone though and Luxembourg celebrated their victory nevertheless.

In 1965 the *Council of Ministers of the European Community* held their first session in Luxembourg, further anchoring the Grand Duchy's status as a capital of Europe. The ministers met three times a year in Luxembourg from then on.

1965 also saw the creation of the *Luxembourg Interconfessional Association*. This body brought together the country's Catholics, Protestants and Jews.

In the same year work was completed on the part canalisation of the Moselle river. This improved the flow of cargo barges up the Rhine as far as Rotterdam. At the same time a new port was opened at Mertert, just north of Grevenmacher where such ships could be docked.

On 5th March 1966 Luxembourg hosted the tenth Eurovision Song Contest at the Villa Louvigny, following the country's victory in 1965. It was hosted by Josiane Shen and was won that year by Austria. The Grand Duchy's own song by Michèle Torr came in 10th.

In the mid 1960s there was a flowering of modern architecture and in April 1964 the *Nouveau Theatre* opened, designed by French architect Alain Bourbonnais. A year later, the *Notre Dame de la Paix* church in Bonnevoie was consecrated. Then, in 1966, the famous *Pont Grand Duchess Charlotte* or *Pont Rouge* (Red Bridge) was opened, connecting the city to the increasingly important Kirchberg Plateau where the new European institutions were housed. At the same time Luxembourg's only sky-scraper, the twenty two storey *European Centre* was opened on the Kirchberg. The Red Bridge and the European Centre almost immediately gained iconic status, featuring on stamps and bank notes and symbolising a new, dynamic Luxembourg. The bridge was indeed a piece of living symbolism, straddling the ancient Pétreuse valley and connecting the old town with the new ultra-modern skyscraper on the Kirchberg. Unlike the other bridges in the city the new red bridge straddled the valley in one giant sweep.

In 1966 future Prime Minister Jacques Santer was beginning his political rise to power and became the parliamentary secretary of the CSV party. Santer would go on to become a leading figure in both Luxembourgish and European politics in future years.

In 1967 Luxair's single F27 was augmented by three more aircraft including a Vickers Viscount. By 1970 the airline had acquired a Caravelle jet and Luxair was beginning to grow into a viable airline, a necessity if Luxembourg was to remain an effective European capital. Having a national airline also boosted international prestige for the Grand Duchy. In March of the same year Luxair created a new company in conjunction with the Icelandic airline Loftleidir and the Scandinavian firm Salen. Loftleider was no stranger to Luxembourg and had been operating a route from the Grand Duchy to New York and Chicago via Keflavic airport in Iceland for some time. This was a vital link for Luxembourg and also provided a cheap route into Europe for countless American backpackers. The new venture was named *Cargolux* becoming one of the Grand Duchy's biggest companies in future years. Luxembourg offered a good location, being in the heart of Europe and *Cargolux* made its first flight in September 1970, to Hong Kong. Its silver and red 747s are now a familiar sight roaring in over the city. Other air routes opened up during the late 1960s, often by lesser known companies and by companies who were looking for a convenient refuelling point. The United Kingdom was served by a company known as *British Eagle,* and its smart planes with their red, white and black livery became a familiar sight in the country. Another airline to service the UK-Luxembourg route was a small company known as *Derby Airlines,* providing a direct link between Luxembourg and Derby. This later became better known as *British Midland.* The Soviet airline, *Aeroflot,* began operating a route from the Irish airport of Shannon to Moscow, using Luxembourg as a base for refuelling and the Finnish flag carrier, *Finnair* also made use of Findel as a stop-over on the route to Spain.

In 1967 there was much excitement when a new supermarket opened in the village of Bereldange. The store, known by the catchy name of *Cactus*, was to become one of the first of a chain of supermarkets and within a decade the chain was one of the biggest food selling outlets in the country.

On the 29th June conscription was ended, making Luxembourg one of the first Western European countries to move over to a professional army.

In 1968 the compulsory teaching of Catholicism was relaxed in secondary schools. Henceforth parents would be allowed to opt their children out of religious education if they wished but despite this new right, an overwhelming majority chose to keep their children in Catholic education.

Another kind of educational facility opened in 1968, when *Miami University* chose Luxembourg as the site of their faculty abroad. The first premises opened in a small centre in the rue du Curé and soon welcomed the first year of American students.

Elections were held in December 1968, returning Pierre Werner as Prime Minister, though this time in coalition with the DP.

In March 1970 Pierre Werner issued a report on a three stage process towards economic and monetary union and a single currency. The report was adopted by all six member states in 1971and a deadline of 1980 was set.

In 1972 a new airport terminal and facilities were opened at Findel. These replaced the by now antiquated post-war buildings a few hundred yards away.

During 1972 the state acquired the ruined castle of Bourscheid for the nation. This was vital if the castle was to be preserved.

In the same year *Actioun Letzebuergesch* was founded, advocating a new spelling system for the language. This was to prove an important force in shaping and promoting the use of Letzebuergesch.

On 25th March 1972 Luxembourg won the *Eurovision Song Contest* for the third time, with the song *Après Toi*, sung by Vicky Leandros. Therefore, on 7th April 1973, Luxembourg hosted the Contest at the *Nouveau Theatre*, overlooking the Pétreuse Valley and the iconic Red Bridge. The show was hosted by Helga Guitton and was marked by heavy security due to the presence of Israel's entry. To put the icing on the cake and give the country even more international prestige, Luxembourg won for a second consecutive year, with *Tu te reconnaitras* by Anne-Marie David. As in 1965 Luxembourg's singer was in fact French.

On a sadder note the photographer Edward Steichen died that year. In his life time he had risen to become one of the world's most renowned photographers.

In 1972 Miami University moved to new premises in rue Goethe, indicating a growing confidence in the success of the university. It was also in 1972 that a young American backpacker arrived at Luxembourg airport, following a long uncomfortable flight from the US via Iceland. It was his first contact with Europe and his name was Bill Bryson. He later recalled the experiences in his book *Neither Here Nor There.*

On 15th June 1974 Gaston Thorn was elected Prime Minister for the DP. In the same year Jacques Santer was elected as leader of the CSV. Both men would later make a big international impact in their own way.

In the late sixties and early seventies the economic outlook had been good and this had attracted a great deal of migrant labour to Luxembourg, notably from Portugal and Italy. However during the mid-1970s Luxembourg's traditional heavy industry was in economic decline. By 1974 the steel industry was in deep crisis, aggravated by the oil crisis in the Middle East. The economic problems therefore made the implementation of the 1971 *Werner Report* on monetary union impossible to achieve. To fight this setback the government introduced new and favourable banking laws in order to attract foreign banks, echoing a similar strategy adopted in the late 1920s. Soon dozens of foreign banks flocked to the Grand Duchy, establishing themselves along the *Boulevard Royale,* and earning the street the title of 'Bankers' Row.'

The economic crisis also led to racial tension between Luxembourgers and the large Portuguese community, which had settled in the Grund and Pfaffenthal areas of the city. The Portuguese community had become by far the largest of Luxembourg's many minorities, with 35%

of all foreigners belonging to the Portuguese community. They formed an underclass of menial workers, with the men working mostly in construction and many women employed as cleaners in private homes and in hotels. The second biggest minority was the Italian community, which accounted for around 20% of resident foreigners. Like the Portuguese they were employed in construction but also in catering, with many going on to open their own businesses. By the early 1970s foreigners constituted 20% of the work force, a drop of nearly 50% from the turn of the century.

In 1975 the veteran politician and former Prime Minister Joseph Bech died. Tributes flooded in from around the world and his contribution to the political landscape of both Luxembourg and Europe were duly noted in the press.

Luxembourg was briefly on centre stage in November 1975 when Gaston Thorn was President of the United Nations Assembly. This illustrates Luxembourg's high international status beyond its size.

In 1976 the unpopular system of Letzebuergesch spelling, introduced by phonetician Jean Feltes, was finally replaced by the more popular system advocated by Henri Rinnen from the group *Actioun Letzebuergesch*. The group tirelessly promoted the new spelling and published a periodical entitled *Eis Sprooch*.

The mid 1970s witnessed an increase in social tensions compounded by recession. One new threat however, came from terrorism, notably from new anarchist factions in Germany and Italy. Whilst not being a target in its own right, Luxembourg was the home to a great many embassies and institutions. Huge queues of cars waiting to cross the borders to and from France and Germany became a frequent sight, at the height of the *Bader Meinhof* terror campaign.

During the mid seventies large numbers of French and German citizens began crossing into Luxembourg to buy cheaper petrol and other consumer goods. It became a frequent occurrence for German vehicles parked in the city and near the airport to be vandalised. Scars from the war were not healing as fast as European leaders may have liked.

In 1977 Luxair acquired a fleet of Being 737s, increasing the range of direct flights from Luxembourg and opening up a new range of package destinations for increasingly adventurous Luxembourgers, as well as developing a wide customer base in neighbouring Belgium, France and Germany. The growth in package tourism was inevitable, as there was virtually no-where for Luxembourgers to spend an extended holiday at home. The size of the country is such that every resort and beauty spot is within a comfortable two hour drive. Traditionally Luxembourgers had flocked to the Belgian coastal resorts until the advent of cheap air travel.

In addition to the usual Mediterranean routes operated by *Luxair* a new company was created using Luxembourg insignia to circumvent the boycott of apartheid in South Africa. Known as *Luxavia*, the airline operated a route from Luxembourg to Johannesburg via Nairobi, using Boeing 707s. South African companies were not allowed to make any stopovers in other African states so the use of a Luxembourg registered company avoided the problem.

In June 1977 the *Luxembourg Society of Wisconsin* was founded in Ozaukee County, an area of dense Luxembourg-American settlement.

Back home, on 16th June 1979, Pierre Werner of the CSV was elected as Prime Minister for the second time, replacing Gaston Thorn. In the same government Jacques Santer became the Minister of Employment and Social Security.

In 1979 the European monetary system was adopted, with the aim of stabilising fluctuations between European currencies, and moving towards the Werner plan of monetary union. This was a key step on the road to the introduction of a single European currency, a cherished goal for many Luxembourgish politicians.

Luxembourg formally abolished the death penalty for all crimes in 1979, although this was a largely symbolic act, thirty years after the last execution had taken place. In the meantime Luxembourg's penal system remained archaic, with prisoners still being housed in the former Neumunster Abbey or *Grund* Prison, until its closure in 1980. The *Grund* Prison was a dreadful and dismal place, with damp, dark cells and lack of modern facilities. Its presence in the heart of the city cast a sinister spell over all who passed-by.

Chapter Ten : Modern times

In 1981, on St Valentine's Day, Prince Henri the eldest son of Grand Duke Jean, married Princess Marie-Therese in some pomp at the Cathedral in Luxembourg City. Later that year crown prince Guillaume was born. These events, and the way in which they were celebrated, demonstrated the continued love of the Luxembourgish people for their royal family.

Another royal wedding took place the following year, on 6th February 1982, when Princess Marie Astride married Christian, Archduke of Austria. This was followed a month later by the marriage of Princess Margaretha to Prince Nicolas of Lichtenstein on 20th March 1982.

On 29th September 1982 Luxembourg suffered its first major civil aviation disaster when a Russian IL62 crashed off the runway into woods, killing ten passengers. The disaster highlighted Luxembourg's rather strange status as a Cold War meeting point when, shortly after the crash, Russian agents made an attempt to get back the airliner's black box.

In addition to boasting an unprofitable air link to Moscow, Luxembourg hosted a disproportionately large Soviet Embassy in a dark and dingy mansion, surrounded by high walls, just outside the village of Dommeldange. A similarly large Chinese embassy was also opened in a nearby chateau. It is possible of course, that the embassy and its diplomatic staff had a slightly larger interest in American troop movements in nearby Germany than in Soviet-Luxembourg relations. Meanwhile American troops remained common visitors to the Grand Duchy, enjoying breaks from service at nearby camps in Western Germany.

As well as American troops, there was an ever growing number of American university students spending a year at the *Miami University*, which moved to the Avenue Monterey in 1982.

On 23rd April 1983 Luxembourg won the *Eurovision Song Contest* for the fifth time, with the song *Si La Vie Est Cadeau* by Corinne Hèrmes. Luxembourg made Eurovision history by winning the contest a total of five times.

In February 1984 a new language law was passed retaining the formal position of French and German as official languages, but also making Luxembourgish the national language for the first time. At the same time, the law formalised the 1976 spelling changes. Henceforth every publication in the language would be required to apply the 1976 spelling rules and civil servants were offered spelling courses. However a clause stated that whilst Letzebuergesch was the national language, it was only to be used as was 'reasonably possible.' French remained the official language of law and German continued as the language in which the government communicated with the general population. Whilst recognising Luxembourgish as the national language, there was no question of downgrading the use of French and German as the official languages of state. This reflected the uneasy tightrope that the Grand Duchy treads between Germanic and French culture, and as a meeting point of European currents. The use of Luxembourgish as sole official lingua franca would have risked making the Grand Duchy a closed society to outsiders. Despite its status as national language Luxembourgish continued to be taught only for one hour a week at school however.

In 1984 the runway at Findel airport was further lengthened making the Grand Duchy a more viable hub for both freight and passenger services.

In the same year the *National Museum of Military History* opened in Diekirch.

On 5th May 1985 Luxembourg hosted the 29th *Eurovision Song Contest* at the *Théatre Municipal*, formally the *Nouveau Théatre*. The show was hosted by Desirée Nosbusch, the youngest presenter in the history of the contest at 19, and was won by Sweden. Luxembourg's own song, *100% Amour,* was sung in French by Sophie Carle and came tenth, despite having been favourite to win.

On 20th July 1984 Jacques Santer was elected Prime Minister, replacing Pierre Werner who retired after a long career. For Santer this was the culmination of a climb to power which had begun in the mid-sixties. Santer also became the governor of the World Bank whilst another Luxembourger, Gaston Thorn, was serving as President of the European Commission. It was during Thorn's time as Commission president that he was called upon to help find a solution to the contentious issue of Britain's EU budget contributions.

Meanwhile veteran Pierre Werner left politics and went on to chair the *Luxembourgish Telecommunications Company*. During the mid-80s CLT, the TV and radio network, began acquiring new franchises in France, Germany, the Netherlands, Sweden and even Poland and Hungary making Luxembourg the centre of a European-wide telecommunication empire.

On 14th June five core EU states signed an agreement at the tiny Luxembourgish town of Schengen, agreeing to phase out border controls between their states. As usual the Grand Duchy helped facilitate groundbreaking European developments. For a tiny landlocked state like Luxembourg the phasing out of border controls was a top priority. It was quite simply impossible for Luxembourg to be either self-sufficient or to live in splendid isolation. Luxembourgers needed to travel freely in order to go to university, make certain purchases or even go to work. In addition many thousands of commuters crossed daily into Luxembourg from towns like Trier in Germany and Arlon in Belgium.

Prince Félix was born in 1984. However the following year, on 9th July 1985, the Grand Duke's mother Grand Duchess Charlotte, the Duchess of Nassau Princess of Bourbon Parma, passed away. This was the occasion of much sadness. Charlotte had ruled the Grand Duchy through one of the most difficult periods in its history, boosting morale with her radio broadcasts and acting as a stablising force in the turbulent times following liberation. The following year however, Prince Louis was born, making a welcome new addition to a growing and young royal family.

On 26th July 1986 a new law was passed, introducing a minimum wage. This had implications for an economy that relied heavily on cheap imported labour, especially in its service sector.

During his term of office Jacques Santer lobbied hard for a vision on political and monetary union, attracting the ire of British Prime Minister Margaret Thatcher who stated that she was inclined to dismiss his rhetoric as 'cloudy and unrealistic aspirations which had no prospect of being implemented.' Santer was re-elected in 1988. It is interesting to reflect on the clash between

Santer and Thatcher nearly twenty years later, in the light of both the introduction of the Euro and the failed attempt at implementing a European Constitution. It is also clear that Luxembourg and Luxembourgish statesmen such as Robert Schuman, Pierre Werner, Gaston Thorn and Jacques Santer have contributed much to the goal of European integration.

In 1989 the seat of the European Parliament moved to a permanent site in Brussels, ending the alternating between Luxembourg and Brussels. This was a blow to Luxembourg, which had lobbied to stop the move and which had built a new hemicycle for the parliament less than a decade earlier. However it made economic sense to keep the parliament in one place and, despite the loss, Luxembourg continued to host a whole range of other EU institutions including the *Court of Justice of the European Union* and the *European Investment Bank*. Nevertheless the loss of the parliamentary sessions, with their hustle and bustle and the attention of the media, was felt.

In the same year Luxembourg celebrated the 150th anniversary of its independence, a big achievement for such a militarily powerless and highly strategic territory at the heart of Western Europe.

In 1989 the renowned Namur café moved to its present location in rue des Capucins. This was the end of an era, ending the prestigious café's presence in the Grand rue. However it allowed for more space and better efficiency and the institution continued to thrive.

In 1990 a massive financial scandal drew the spotlight on the country's banking institutions, when employees at the *Bank of Credit and Commerce International* were caught laundering drug money. This was an embarrassment for the Grand Duchy, and brought calls for change from some of Luxembourg's EU partners.

Over the border in Belgium, speakers of Letzebuergesch received official recognition when the *Council of the French Community of Belgium* passed a decree on the protection and promotion of minority languages in 1990. For the first time, Letzebuergesch speakers in Belgium could receive some of their secondary education in their native tongue. There was also provision for some radio broadcasts in the language.

Meanwhile in the United States, the *Luxembourg Heritage Society* was formed, with the aim of fostering links between Luxembourg and America.

In the same year, 1990, there was excitement when the remains of a Roman villa where excavated at the village of Helmsange, casting light on how the Romans had lived in the area.

In 1991 the Grand Duchy introduced a new taxation system with lower taxes. This was an attempt to kick start a sluggish economy, slowed by German reunification and the subsequent problems this caused for Luxembourg's main trading partner.

Princess Alexandra was born the same year, as usual a source of national celebration.

On 2nd July 1992 Luxembourg ratified the Maastricht Treaty but added a get-out clause preventing other EU citizens from voting in Luxembourgish local elections. By the early 1990s Luxembourg had a higher percentage of non-nationals living in its borders than any other EU state, with the number standing at nearly 40%. Nevertheless it was out of character for a normally so-wholeheartedly European Luxembourg to insist on a get-out clause.

In March 1992, and until August 1993, Luxembourgish troops under Belgian command were deployed in Croatia. This underlined Luxembourg's commitment to common military security. It was however largely symbolic considering the number of troops involved.

In 1992 the last of the future Grand Duke Henri's five children, Prince Sébastien, was born.

In May 1992 Marion Welter and *Kontinent* sang a song in Letzebuergesch at the *Eurovision Song Contest* in Malmo, Sweden. This was the second time the world had heard a song in the language, the first time being 1960. The song came second from last.

In 1993, after years of pressure from inhabitants of the Pfaffenthal area, suicide barriers were erected along the Pont Rouge. Since its construction in 1966 over one hundred people had jumped from it. Suicide remained a concern in the country, being one of the most common causes of death amongst certain age groups, and ranking fourteenth in the world. It is not clear why suicide should be so high in a country with so few problems. However, some social commentators have attributed the phenomenon to a lack of challenge and daily struggle.

In 1992 the age of consent for gays was fixed at 16 under changes to articles 372-378 of the penal code. This brought Luxembourg into line with European norms. Homosexuality was a subject that had never really been in the public eye, with the tiny gay scene being found only in small windowless bars. There were virtually no openly gay public figures or organisations, and in schools Catholic education did not allow for open debate on the subject. Nevertheless the Luxembourgish government had not engaged in any major witch hunts or active persecution.

Luxembourg had remained tolerant up to a point but life did, and still does, revolve around the extended family.

In 1993 Luxembourg came under EU pressure to implement new financial laws to prevent the relocation of numerous banks to the Grand Duchy. This was a source of concern, bearing in mind the importance of the banking sector to the country's economy.

In 1994 Luxembourg became a *UNESCO World Heritage Site.*

In the same year the Grand Duchy celebrated the 50th anniversary of its liberation in the Second World War. The scars remained close to the surface, with nearly every family having grandparents who remembered the experience at first hand. In addition most towns or villages have a memorial naming the martyrs of their community and the north of the country is rich in preserved American tanks, which serve as memorials. Nazism remains utterly taboo with very little in the way of a skinhead culture or rightwing demagogues. Even toyshops vet the covers of models, rubbing out any swastikas on the packets.

On 24th September 1994 Prince Guillaume married Sibilla Weiller to the joy of Luxembourgers everywhere.

On 20th January 1995 Jean-Claude Juncker became Prime Minister, replacing Jacquues Santer who had been the leader since 1984. Once again the CSV remained in power. In turn Jacques Santer became the President of the European Commission and it is under his presidency that the EU took the two historic steps of introducing the Euro and preparing for the accession of the former Communist states in the East. Santer was actually a compromise choice for the post however, as Britain had used its veto to scuttle the Belgian Jean-Luc Dehaene.

In December 1996 Luxembourgish troops participated in the *United Nations Stablization Force,* SFOR, and carried out their first mission in January 1997. This consisted of protecting the route from Split to Visoko in the Former Yugoslavia. Once again, the role was largely symbolic, but it continued to underscore Luxembourg's commitment to European security.

In 1997 the film *American Werewolf in Paris* was filmed in Luxembourg. Luxembourg, and especially the Grund quarter of the city, became an increasingly attractive film set with *Girl With The Pearl Earring* being filmed in the city five years later. The Grund was dark and moody and well suited to period dramas.

The Grund had traditionally been a slum as well as a traditional immigrant quarter. However, during the late nineties it became gentrified and expensive, with real estate prices rocketing.

The Miami University, already a long-established presence in the country, invested heavily in 1997 and acquired the Chateau at Differdange for its campus.

In April 1998 Luxembourg and Belgium set up the *Belgium Luxembourg Battle Group,* BELUBG, under British command and Luxembourgish forces were deployed to Tomislavgrad as part of this force. Their mission was to provide a military deterrent, to stop looting and hostage taking and to oversee the implementation of the Dayton accord in the former Yugoslavia.

In 1998 Luxembourg was admitted as an associate of the international cricketing body, the ICC. However, this mostly reflected the growing Anglo-Saxon presence in the Grand Duchy rather than a burgeoning interest in the sport amongst Luxembourgers.

In June 1998 the *European Central Bank* came into being to manage the new European Euro currency. At the same time the *Banque Centrale du Luxembourg* was created to work alongside it.

In 1999 the *Belgium Luxembourg Kosovo Battalion* was set up for peace keeping duties in the troubled area, further cementing Luxembourg's military role.

In March 1999 there were reports that European Commission President Jacques Santer was close to a nervous breakdown, after he and his fellow commissioners were forced to resign over allegations of mismanagement. This arose when the French government insisted that all the European Commissioners take the flack, instead of allowing the French commissioner Edith Cresson to take the blame alone. This in turn led to talk of bigger EU states throwing their weight around to dominate the Luxembourgish EU president. Santer had been appointed president of the Commission with the backing of British Prime Minister John Major, who saw Jacques Santer as something of an ally.

In 2000 Henri became Grand Duke, succeeding his father Grand Duke Jean, who abdicated in his favour. This move mirrored that taken by the Grand Duke's own mother decades earlier. Like then, it allowed the Grand Ducal family to remain young and dynamic.

On 30th July 1999 a Grand Ducal decree standardised reforms to the spelling of Letzebuergesch, following years of campaigning by interested groups.

In January 2000 Luxembourgish troops withdrew from the former Yugoslavia, marking the end of the Grand Duchy's peace keeping role.

In the same year the CLT radio and TV network

merged with the British company *Pearson TV* to form the *RTL Group*. This resulted in the control of twenty six TV stations, twenty four radio stations and an audience of 250 million viewers in thirty nine countries.

In 2000 the *gendarmerie* merged with the police to form the *Police Grand Ducale*. For over a hundred years the two forces had been separate and distinct, with the former being almost militaristic in its deployment. The move was designed to bring better cooperation and efficiency to the police service.

On 1st June the peace of the Grand Duchy was shattered when Neji Bejaoui took forty children hostage at a day care centre in the town of Wasserbillig. Bejaoui, an unemployed and bitter loner from Tunisia, had been struggling with mental illness for a while. This was compounded when his own children were taken into care. He had scandalised his Luxembourgish neighbours by beating his wife and even dragging her through the streets of Manternach at knifepoint. He chose the day care centre as his target as he blamed its staff for informing the authorities about his condition, ultimately having his children taken from him.

Many of the children were Portuguese, prompting the Portuguese ambassador to offer his country's assistance. German elite police were also on hand. The police pretended to set up a press interview for Bejaoui who then emerged with three children, demanding a plane to take him to Libya. At this point Bejaoui was shot in the head at point blank range, by a police officer posing as a journalist, but later recovered in hospital. Bejaoui had been armed with a gun, a hand grenade and a knife. The *International Federation of Journalists* condemned the

Grand Ducal police for the action, which it described as 'unethical.' Nevertheless all the children emerged safely from the situation, which could easily have become a tragedy.

The incident brought into sharp relief issues relating to foreigners in Luxembourg. This unease was partly responsible for moves towards a fresh look at the issue and on 24th July a new nationality law was passed. Children born in Luxembourg to foreign parents would be eligible for citizenship provided they had lived in the country for five years or more. In addition they would be required to give up their existing citizenship and pass a test in Letzebuergesch, French and German. Other foreign residents would need to live in the country for five consecutive years and pass a proficiency test in the three languages. A high level of mastery of Letzebuergesch would excuse them from learning French and German. The high level of status given to Letzebuergesch contrasts to earlier years when the language was denied any formal status at all and French was the official language of government. There were similarities with a similar nationality act in Denmark where applicants for citizenship or even social security would need to have mastered the local language. It had the effect of making Luxembourgish citizenship more difficult to acquire, the language being unused outside the country, in contrast to German, British or French which are widely spoken all over the world.

During 2001 the Moselle valley produced one of its best ever wine vintages, reinforcing the country's role as a major wine producer.

On 1st January 2002 Luxembourg and other core EU countries abandoned their national currencies and adopted the Euro. On 28th February the Luxembourgish Franc ceased to be legal tender. For Luxembourg this was perhaps less of a national sacrifice than for other countries, such as the Netherlands or France, for whom the currency had long been a symbol of their national sovereignty. After all, for most of its existence as a state Luxembourg's economy and currency had been pegged to other states, for example the Prussian *Thaler* or the Belgian Franc.

On 24th June 2002 Pierre Werner died at the age of 88. Pierre Werner had been one of Luxembourg's longest serving Prime Ministers and was often described as the father of the Euro for his work on monetary union in the early 1970s. Tributes flooded in from all over the world and the Grand Duke personally expressed his sadness. It is fitting that Werner lived long enough to see the creation of his dream, the Euro.

In July 2002 the Grand Duchy became the first country outside France to become the starting point of the world famous *Tour de France* bike race, illustrating the increasing insignificance of borders between Schengen states.

On 6th November Luxembourg suffered its second civil aviation disaster when a Luxair F20 crashed in poor weather, killing nearly all twenty passengers on board. The plane had been making its final approach into Luxembourg on a flight from Berlin in very poor conditions at around 10.15 in the morning. The Belgian airforce sent three helicopters to the scene at the request of the Luxembourgish authorities and this move illustrates the tight co-operation between the two countries.

By 2002 Luxair had begun to acquire newer and slicker jet aircraft, hoping to develop Findel as a European hub airport with smooth and speedy connections to other EU states.

In 2003 the world famous internet book trader Amazon.com relocated to Luxembourg, providing a welcome boost to the economy.

The following year, on 31st July 2004, a new government under Jean-Claude Junker was sworn in, following a shift in the coalition. The liberals left and were replaced by socialists. This was a marked change in the generally placid political climate.

2004 saw the construction of two blue sky scrappers on the Kirschberg plateau, to house Eurocrats from the newly expanded EU. Work was also underway on the new *Salle Philharmonique de Luxembourg* and the *Musee d'Art Moderne Grand Duc Jean*.

Across the Atlantic, the *Luxembourg American Cultural Society* was formed that year, with the goal of preserving Luxembourg's heritage and culture, and of fostering ties. Plans were presented for the construction of a *Luxembourg American Cultural Centre,* in Wisconsin, as part of a wider development known as *New Luxembourg*. The plans include a museum, dedicated to American Luxembourgish heritage. This is to be housed in a barn, which was built by a Luxembourgish immigrant in the late nineteenth century.

In November 2004 gays and lesbians were given a limited number of partnership rights under the *Declaration de Partenariat,* including pension rights. This followed a European wide trend but fell short of full marriage, due in part to the traditionally Catholic nature of the Grand Duchy. This contrasts to the Netherlands and Belgium, both of which introduced full gay marriage and did so much earlier.

On 5th July 2005 Luxembourg commemorated the sixtieth anniversary of the Holocaust. A monument was unveiled by vice-Prime Minister Jean Asselborn, along with the Great Rabbi, at the village of Cinqfontaines in the north of the country. The village was chosen as the location of the memorial as it was there, at the convent, that hundreds of Jews, roughly 30% of the Jewish population, were held before being deported.

On 10th July 2005 Luxembourg voted to ratify the EU constitution in a referendum, despite the rejection of the treaty in France and the Netherlands. However, for a country which is so much at the heart of Europe the 56% Yes vote was astoundingly low and it was a close run thing for Prime Minister Junker, who had staked his future on a Yes vote. Many of the No voters expressed concerns about immigration and unemployment.

Conclusion

We are now at the end of our story. We have seen the growth of a castle fort into a dukedom whose strength stretched at one time as far as Central Europe. We have traced the vacillatations in fortune of various dynasties who have ruled the area, as well as the lot of the people who have suffered from famine, plague and occupation, followed by industrialisation and more occupation. Yet despite the ebb and flow of borders, the erection of castles and rule by foreign leaders there has been a remarkable continuity and spirit in the Luxembourgish people. This is a people whose language developed in the fifth century and whose food and wine have been famed even since Roman times; a people who have withstood the attempts of the French, Belgian and German states to annex them, often with great personal courage. It is a country which has absorbed and adapted wave after wave of cultural innovations in architecture, economics, and international politics, and in recent years has been at the forefront of the new Europe. And through all of these changes life continues peacefully and traditionally. In recent years there has been a growing self-confidence in Luxembourgers and a new willingness to promote their language, to influence international politics and even to send troops abroad. Occasionally Luxembourg surprises the world, giving them a famous artist or statesman or winning the *Eurovision Song Contest* five times. Otherwise Luxembourgers are content to enjoy their tiny country and ask only that people remember their national motto: *mir welle bleive wat mir sin,* we wish to remain what we are.

The End

About the Author

Andrew Reid is a lecturer in English and spent his childhood in Luxembourg. He has an MA in Victorian Studies and now lives in Loughton, Essex.

Printed in the United Kingdom by
Lightning Source UK Ltd., Milton Keynes
140980UK00001B/301/A